Village and Farm

Cottages.

Village and Farm Cottages

A Victorian Stylebook of 1856

With a New Introduction by

David Schuyler

AMERICAN LIFE FOUNDATION

1982

ISBN: 0-89257-008-3

THE AMERICAN LIFE FOUNDATION is a non-profit, educational institution specializing in the acquisition and dissemination of
knowledge through publications. Open to the study of all aspects
of American life, it is especially interested in the relationships of
things and ideas and how the social functions of artifacts from
the past relate to those of today. Recently, it has been repub-
lishing many nineteenth-century stylebooks about architecture
and the decorative arts to assist old house owners and other
preservationists. For a free listing write:

American Life Books, Box 349, Watkins Glen, NY 14891.

INTENDED to be a sequel to the work of A. J. Downing, this book was first published in 1856—four years after Downing had drowned in the aftermath of a steamboat explosion in the Hudson River. *Village and Farm Cottages*, by New York architects Henry W. Cleaveland and the Backus Brothers, matches a no nonsense "scientific" treatise on town planning, the environment, landscaping, gardening, house planning, materials, construction, style, ventilation, interiors, and house painting with 100 delightful views, plans, initials, and vignettes.

John Crosby Freeman
Director of Publications
March, 1982

David Schuyler

Village and Farm Cottages: The Ideology of
Domesticity

UNLIKE THE WRITINGS of Andrew Jackson Downing, whose popularity merited the publication of numerous editions in his lifetime and which remain readily available today, *Village and Farm Cottages* has long been neglected. In part this is because of the authors' relative anonymity—the names of Henry W. Cleaveland, William Backus, and Samuel D. Backus are unfamiliar to all but the most assiduous contemporary readers—and in part because their book faced rigorous competition from the works of other writers similarly attempting to claim the mantle as tastemaker to the nation, a position left vacant by Downing's untimely death in 1852.

But *Village and Farm Cottages* is an important book, one that addresses some of the major cultural issues of the 1850s. True, the sectional traumas that threatened the nation are absent, but so they were from most books devoted to the principles of design published during that decade. Instead, Cleaveland and the Backus brothers took up a different battle, the nineteenth-century crusade to improve domestic architecture and to enshrine the home as the bastion of culture. The key to this reformist program, the ideology of domesticity, was a more or less coherent philosophy of the role of art and taste in civilizing American society. Proponents of domesticity, who included prominent ministers, feminists, and architects, shared a world view essentially middle class in orientation and New England in origin. Theirs was admittedly a conservative attempt to reinforce the values of home and family in a society wracked by the enormous changes attendant to urbanization and industrialization.

Central to the ideology of domesticity was the belief, best expressed by the Congregational theologian Timothy Dwight, that the "perception of beauty and deformity" was the first and most permanent influence on the mind. Dwight's assertion that a well-designed building would awaken taste even in the most "grovelling, brutish character" had as a corollary Horace Bushnell's conviction that in the home parents exercised over their children an "unconscious influence" so powerful as to be an absolute force. This combination of environment and psychology made it imperative that parents—and especially the women who assumed primary responsibility for nurture—provide the familial setting that would enhance child development. At stake in this crusade was nothing less than the fate of the nation: Cleaveland and the Backus brothers considered the reformed domestic environment the battleground on which the forces of civilization would conquer barbarism and social disorder. And the reading public eagerly sought their advice: *Village and Farm Cottages* was reprinted three times in the thirteen years following its initial appearance in 1856.[1]

Like Downing, Cleaveland and the Backus brothers offered three compelling reasons why the reform of domestic architecture was a national priority. First, they asserted, the "character" of a well-designed home was a measure of man's progress from the animal state to "civilization and refinement" and gave irrefutable evidence of man's "higher nature." Second, they pointed out, there is "an important moral influence" in the household, an inexorable force "by which men are to be transferred from the government of Sense and Passion, to that of Reason and Affections." By this account, "every improvement in the abodes of men, which renders them more neat, comfortable, and pleasing, contributes not only to physical enjoyment, but to mental and moral advancement." Third, because the family was "the foundation, the beginning of any society," the authors believed that every advance in the design of houses would nurture domestic associations and thereby strengthen the social order.[2]

Cleaveland and the Backus brothers addressed their prescriptions for improving the home to a specific audience, "mechanics and tradesmen of moderate circumstances, the small farmer, and the laboring man generally." Because the structure of the American economy rewarded labor while the cost of land and building materials remained comparatively inexpensive, the authors rejected the "evils of hired abodes." Instead, they asserted, ownership of a house was within the reach of every industrious man, and at a cost no greater than that paid for inferior rental accommodations. To this end *Village and Farm Cottages* presented plans for what its authors considered a "humbler class" of dwellings than those illustrated in Downing's publications—cottages of one and two stories, small in scale, modest in cost, and operated by members of the household without the assistance of maids or cooks.[3]

Despite the apparent simplicity of their cottages, Cleaveland and the Backus brothers demanded that such houses conform to all the requisites of domesticity. The well-designed home must, they insisted, be located on a healthful site, be adapted to the uses intended, be truthful in the use of materials, express purpose, and express the individuality of its inhabitants. Their floor plans provided for efficiency in the service and maintenance of the house, for adequate storage, and, when possible, for the introduction of interior plumbing and water closets. To these prescriptions the authors added advice on the proper landscaping of the residence and arrangement of the flower or vegetable garden. No aspect of the domestic environment escaped their attention, for only in such a carefully contrived and rational setting could the associations of home and family reach their fullest potential.

The foundation of this attempt to civilize American society by reforming domestic architecture was the principle of imitation. Downing, who considered imitation one of the foremost characteristics of the American people, believed that well-designed homes would awaken in people an appreciation for orderly surroundings and lead them to improve their own dwellings. Similarly, Cleaveland and the Backus brothers pointed out that the "example of one good house is sometimes followed by an improvement in the style and taste of a whole village." And like Downing, who ordained his followers "apostles of culture," the authors of *Village and Farm Cottages* charged their readers to provide the examples of architectural excellence worthy of imitation by their countrymen.[4]

The best possible location for such homes, of course, was a non-urban setting. Together with most promoters of the ideology of domesticity, Cleaveland and the Backus brothers subscribed to a romantic hostility toward cities. They condemned the "evils of tenement life"—shabby accommodations, the appalling prevalence of disease and high mortality rates, the proximity of the various corruptions of the city—and celebrated the advantages of a residence in the country. There parents could rear their children "away from the dangers and temptations, the unnatural excitements and morbid stimulants, the thousand habits and haunts of vice, with which the city abounds." For surely the task of reforming American society could best be accomplished in a rural home, amidst surroundings conducive to health and morality.[5]

Although the increasing economic dominance of cities threatened the practicality of the idealized rural life they advocated, Cleaveland and the Backus brothers grasped the significance of changes that promoted the establishment of suburban villages. The suburb, they explained, was a "comparatively recent invention to relieve the hard-working and severely pressed population of our cities." According to the authors, improvements in steamboats and the extension of railroads made travel between rural and urban areas fast and inexpensive, thereby bringing country and city closer together. These new transportation systems obviated the need for workers to live near their places of employment and enabled them to build houses on the urban periphery, where land was cheaper and the environment more appropriate to domesticity.[6]

The authors of *Village and Farm Cottages* also offered advice on the proper arrangement of suburban communities. Like Downing, who had castigated the use of the gridiron in a rural setting, they rejected the idea that in a suburb the streets "should all run in straight lines, and cross at right angles." In their estimation, the rectangular street plan was acceptable only in cities, where exorbitant property values necessitated maximum use of available space. But in the country, where land was plentiful, the values of domesticity were more compelling than "mathematical economy." Accordingly, the authors recommended that streets and roads be curvilinear and conform to the topography of the site. Moreover, as Downing had advocated in "Our Country Villages," his theoretical program for suburban development, and as Frederick Law Olmsted and Calvert Vaux would propose to the Riverside Improvement Company in 1868, Cleaveland and the Backus brothers urged the "reservation for public use and enjoyment of some open space in every village." [7]

Village and Farm Cottages is also important because it reflects the increasing influence of John Ruskin's theories on American architecture. The authors' allusion to the "greatest of modern writers on art" undoubtedly referred to Ruskin, whose books— *The Seven Lamps of Architecture* (1849) and *The Stones of Venice* (1853)—"fell like bombs into the camps of Classical and Renaissance architecture." Throughout the pages of their book, Cleaveland and the Backus brothers incorporated ideas of truth, beauty, and expression, ideas first clearly formulated in Ruskin's writings and popularized in a format "adapted" to North America by Downing.[8]

Village and Farm Cottages is one of the most important architectural pattern books published in the United States at the middle of the nineteenth century. In offering suggestions on the proper design, landscaping, and location of the home, its authors attempted to provide the models that would improve residential architecture and create the familial surroundings most conducive to domesticity. Undoubtedly Cleaveland and the Backus brothers hoped that the publication of this book would result in an increase in the number of clients seeking their advice. More importantly, the authors defined their role as arbiters of taste as honorable: "he who improves the dwelling-houses of a people in relation to their comforts, habits, and morals," they reasoned, "makes a benignant and lasting reform at the very foundation of society." [9]

David Schuyler
Franklin and Marshall College

NOTES

1 On the culture of domesticity see Carl N. Degler, At Odds: Women and the Family in America from the Revolution to the Present (New York, 1980), Kathryn Kish Sklar, Catharine Beecher; A Study in American Domesticity (New Haven, 1973), and David P. Handlin, The American Home: Architecture and Society, 1815–1915 (Boston, 1979). For Timothy Dwight's remarks, quoted from Travels in New England and New York (1822), see infra, pp. 47–48. See also Horace Bushnell, Views of Christian Nurture and Subjects Adjacent Thereto (1847; reprint ed., Delmar, N. Y., 1975), pp. 6, 183–85. For information on the subsequent publication of Village and Farm Cottages see Henry-Russell Hitchcock, American Architectural Books, new ed. (New York, 1976), p. 25.

2 Infra, pp. 2–3, and the authors' preface, n. p.; compare with A. J. Downing, The Architecture of Country Houses (New York, 1850), pp. xix–xx.

3 Infra, authors' preface, n. p., and p. 11.

4 Ibid., pp. 46, 171. On the principle of imitation see [A. J. Downing], "On the Moral Influence of Good Houses," The Horticulturist, and Journal of Rural Art and Rural Taste 2, no. 8 (Feb. 1848): 346–47, and [Downing], "Trees, in Towns and Villages," ibid. 1, no. 9 (Mar. 1847): 395.

5 Infra, pp. 6–16.

6 Ibid., p. 17. On the early history of the suburb see Kenneth T. Jackson, "The Crabgrass Frontier: 150 Years of Suburban Growth in America," in The Urban Experience: Themes in American History, ed. Raymond Mohl and James F. Richardson (Belmont, Ca., 1973). On the tendency of workers to live near their places of employment see David Ward, Cities and Immigrants: A Geography of Change in Nineteenth-century America (New York, 1971), p. 107. See also Joel Arthur Tarr, "From City to Suburb: The 'Moral' Influence of Transportation Technology," in American Urban History: An Interpretative Reader With Commentaries, ed. Alexander B. Callow, 2nd ed. (New York, 1973), and George R. Taylor, "The Beginnings of Mass Transportation in Urban America, Part I," Smithsonian Journal of History 1 (Summer 1966): 35–50.

7 Infra, pp. 17–19; A. J. Downing, "Our Country Villages," reprinted in Rural Essays, By A. J. Downing. Edited, With a Memoir of the Author, by George William Curtis; and a Letter to his Friends, by Fredrika Bremer (New York, 1853), pp. 236–43; Olmsted, Vaux & Company, Preliminary Report Upon the Proposed Village at Riverside, Near Chicago (New York, 1868), p. 25.

8 Infra, p. 65. see also Roger B. Stein, John Ruskin and Aesthetic Thought in America, 1840–1900 (Cambridge, 1967).

9 Infra, p. 4.

Village and Farm Cottages.

Village and Farm Cottages.

Illustrated with One Hundred Engravings.

NEW YORK:

D. APPLETON AND COMPANY.

1856

Village and Farm Cottages.

THE REQUIREMENTS OF

AMERICAN VILLAGE HOMES

CONSIDERED AND SUGGESTED;

WITH DESIGNS FOR SUCH HOUSES

OF MODERATE COST.

BY

HENRY W. CLEAVELAND, WILLIAM BACKUS, AND SAMUEL D. BACKUS.

NEW YORK:

D. APPLETON AND COMPANY,

846 & 348 BROADWAY.

1856.

PREFACE.

IN preparing the following pages of designs and hints, we have had in view a class, numerous and important in every community, but specially so in ours—comprehending mechanics and tradesmen of moderate circumstances, the small farmer, and the laboring man generally. Fortunately for these, labor here is still remunerative, while land and building material are abundant and cheap. A modest home, which he may call his own, is beyond the reach of no capable and industrious man. It is a laudable ambition which prompts him to strive for such an object; and in no way, perhaps, can we serve him and his family more effectually than by encouraging his efforts.

We have endeavored to provide the villager of limited means with a plan for his small house, in which strict economy shall be combined with comfort, good looks, and substantial value.

Convenience, facility in doing the family work, and pleasantness of internal aspect and arrangements, were our first aim. In the building and furnishing of a house, surely, if any where, charity should begin at home. Over all other considerations, the pleasure and advantage of its future occupants claim undeniable precedence.

But true charity does not stop where it begins. In the minor, as well as greater moralities, it respects the rights of others, and gladly ministers not only to their wants, but to their tastes. To improve the form, decoration, and finish of the exterior, and the general character of its surroundings—though a secondary consideration—is by no means an unimportant one. And, hence, we have given to this point very careful attention.

We believe that every improvement in the abodes of men, which renders them more neat, comfortable, and pleasing, contributes not only to physical enjoyment, but to mental and moral advancement. This idea, so important and encouraging, is presented more fully in the book.

The admirable publications of the much lamented Downing gave a new and lasting impulse to the architecture of our country residences. We shall feel rewarded if we may be considered to have done something in the same direction, with regard to an humbler class of structures. .

In the designs here offered, and in the remarks which precede and accompany them, we have endeavored to exhibit correct principles in art, and to foster a pure and just taste. In these alone is to be found the corrective power that can check the universal tendency to imitation,—a passion which almost invariably prefers the meretricious to the true.

In every part of the work we have endeavored to secure accuracy and thoroughness. The perspectives have all been delineated on the blocks by ourselves,—having been reduced from working drawings, executed with mathematical exactness.

If we have introduced, sometimes, topics and considerations not strictly applicable to village cottages like these of ours, our apology is, that we address men accustomed to read and think,—men of energy and progress,—not a few of whom will build better houses one of these days. The lesson taught, if it be good, will not be thrown away.

For presenting some other matters here, which are not exactly architectural, we have no better reason to give than that we regard them as important, and believe they will be useful.

Most of the landscapes, foliage, etc., the initial cuts, and other embellishments, are due to the skillful pencil of Mr. F. A. Chapman, and speak their own praise. We believe the same will be said of Mr. Howland's engraving.

NOTICE.

FOR the convenience of such as may wish to build after any of the designs in this work, the Authors have prepared careful, lithographed working drawings and printed specifications for each. These comprise every thing necessary to enable any competent workman fully to understand the plans. They will be forwarded, together with blank forms of contract, by mail, on receipt of a special application, and remittance, at the following rates :—For any one of the first ten designs, $3. For Numbers 11, 12, 13, and 14, $4 each. For the last ten, $5 each.

They will be pleased to answer any inquiries that may arise, and to make such suggestions relative to the execution of the designs in particular localities, as the circumstances of the case, and the information furnished, shall seem to require.

Address CLEAVELAND & BACKUS BROTHERS,
Architects, 41 Wall Street, New York.

CONTENTS.

— • • • —

CHAPTER I.

THE HOUSE CONSIDERED IN ITS INFLUENCE ON THE OCCUPANTS.

CHAPTER II.

THE VALUE OF A PERMANENT HOME.

CHAPTER III.

HOME IN THE COUNTRY.

CHAPTER IV.

THE VILLAGE.

CHAPTER V.

THE CHOICE OF A LOT.

CHAPTER VI.

THE ADOPTION OF A PLAN.

CHAPTER VII.

PRINCIPLES AS APPLIED TO DETAILS.

CONTENTS.

CHAPTER VIII.

COTTAGES OF ONE STORY.

CHAPTER IX.

COTTAGES OF ONE STORY AND ATTIC.

CHAPTER X.

HILL-SIDE COTTAGES.

CHAPTER XI.

HOUSES OF TWO STORIES.

CHAPTER XII.

FARM-HOUSES.

CHAPTER XIII.

DOUBLE COTTAGES.

CHAPTER XIV.

INTERIORS.

CHAPTER XV.

HINTS ON CONSTRUCTION.

CONTENTS.

CHAPTER XVI.

THE IMPROVEMENT OF GROUNDS.

CHAPTER XVII.

THE GARDEN.

VILLAGE AND FARM COTTAGES.

CHAPTER I.

THE HOUSE CONSIDERED IN ITS INFLUENCE ON THE OCCUPANTS.

THE countless varieties of animal existence are hardly more distinct in size, form, and color, than in the character of their respective habitations. From the natural cave where the wolf hides, to the artistic house of the beaver ;—from the caterpillar's tangled home, to the waxen and paper cells of the bee and wasp ;—from the eagle's rude aerie on the bare cliff, to the pendent and symmetric shelter of the oriole—the range is wide indeed. And yet, through all these gradations, an unerring instinct prompts each species to find, or to construct, such an abode for themselves, or such a nursery for their young, as their peculiar natures and habits demand. But the operations of instinct, though perfect, are necessarily limited and unchanging. Of progress they know nothing. The first humming-bird of Eden cradled and fed her offspring in a nest, which differed probably in no particular from thousands that might be seen to-day in the groves of Cuba or Cashmere.

With man the case is far different. His wants and capabilities are so much more numerous, and complex, and various, than those of the brute creation ; his powers of thought and action are so incomparably superior, that we might expect to find some of the most striking proofs of his higher nature in the structures which he rears for himself. And such is the fact. The degree in which he has been raised by civilization and refinement above the unreasoning animal, is shown in nothing more clearly than in the character of his dwelling. We are not surprised when we find the poor savage of the North, burrowing in an underground cabin, compared with which the homes of the mole and marmot shine as models of neatness and comfort. But we may well wonder when we see families, among people calling themselves civilized and Christian, content to dwell in hovels hardly good enough for swine. Can we doubt, when we behold such cases, that the dwellings of men often exert a powerful influence on their habits and character? Certainly, no race, or community, or family, or individual, while dwelling contentedly in filth and discomfort, can be called respectable, or deemed happy.

Regarded in this light, human dwellings acquire new consequence. They become an important moral influence ; one of the means by which men are to be transferred from the government of Sense and Passion, to that of Reason and the Affections. Their improvement takes rank, at once, among the moral reforms, and is prompted by motives higher than mere comfort, or fashion, or pecuniary advantage. The point is an important one, and deserves a moment's attention.

The relations which men bear to one another are among the most efficient of the influences that mould their character. Society is a network of closely interwoven interests, wants, and dependencies. From these come, not only our various occupations and means of living, but nearly all our tastes and sympathies, and many of our richest enjoyments. Common sense and all experience tell us that man was not made to live in the hermit's cave, or in the cynic's tub. The most successful seeker of happiness is not he who has reduced his wants to the smallest possible number. The Being who made us with capacities for enjoyment, so numerous and varied, could never have meant that the greater part of them should rust unused. We may be all the happier by having many wants, provided they are not improper in their kind, not imperious in their demands, and not beyond our ability to gratify them.

The pattern, the foundation, the beginning of all society, is the Family. In this institution, to which, more than to governments or to great men, the progress of humanity may be traced, centre those ties which connect the individual with the community at large. Here we first learn that we are mutually dependent and reciprocally responsible. This connection, which begins and ends only with life, and which holds its members by bonds so strong and yet so delicate, must powerfully affect, for good or ill, all who are within its influence. Hence the importance of those means and instruments by which its power is modified. Prominent among these stands the *home;* an idea so blended with all the affections and associations of the *family,* that the terms are almost convertible.

Every enlightened plan for the advancement of family influences and of society in general, will include among its earliest efforts the improvement of dwellings ; and this, not only in respect of physical comfort, but of that aid which they can be made to render in the suggestion of salutary associations and the formation of desirable habits. When Architecture contributes to such an object, she may justly claim the highest praise. Splendid monuments, temples, and palaces do, indeed, exhibit the wonders of invention and tasteful skill. They proclaim the wealth, and gratify the pride, of individuals and of nations. They may act as a beneficial stimulus to the public taste. But he who improves the dwelling-houses of a people in relation to their comforts, habits, and morals, makes a benignant and lasting reform at the very foundation of society.

That the dwelling should most effectually contribute to such a purpose, its location and its arrangements should be, as far as possible, adapted to the condition, employment, habits, and character of the family. And not only are the adult members to be thought of. The interests of the young should especially be consulted. By all means let the abodes of infancy and youth be made commodious and attractive. These, however humble, may teach lessons of neatness and order ; they may and should inspire a regard for comfort and decorum. While the mind and heart are fresh and tender, let the love of parents and kindred be combined with that of place ; the love, to wit, of one's own house and fireside, of garden, tree, and prospect. Thus may you contribute toward rendering the homes of the people not only nurseries of filial and fraternal affection, but the earliest and best schools of obedience and duty, of patriotism and piety.

CHAPTER II.

THE VALUE OF A PERMANENT HOME.

E have endeavored to show that an important purpose ought to dictate and control all the arrangements of a home. But such a purpose can be fulfilled only where the dwelling is permanent. With the habitation which we feel to be but temporary,—our continued occupancy of which depends, perhaps, on another's will, unadapted to the peculiar wants of the family, and unendeared by the associations of long familiarity, it is hardly possible to connect ideas of *domestic* comfort, and quiet, and repose. For the full attainment of these benefits, and of those higher ones to which we have alluded, the dwelling should be *owned* by its occupants. This practice is so general, except in large cities, and has in itself so much to commend it, that it may seem to some almost needless to urge its importance here. Among our rural population, and in the smaller towns, almost every man owns the house in which he lives. In cities, the case generally is far otherwise. There, living in miserable hired tenements, we find the men of small means, the artisans and laborers,—almost the whole of that large and important class who depend on daily toil for their daily support, and who certainly most need the comforts and influences of a permanent and pleasant home. That so many of these seem contented with their lot, and make no effort to exchange lodgings, so uncomfortable and so unfit, for suitable dwellings of their own, is a strange fact, and (making all allowance for the difficulties and apparent hopelessness of their condition) can be accounted for only by the paralyzing influence which such abodes exert upon their occupants.

As it is this class, particularly, which we hope to reach and to benefit, it seems proper to dwell for a moment on the nature and evils of tenant-life as it prevails in our large towns.

Of all the abodes rented by Avarice to Necessity, the lowest and worst are the sunken basements, the inhabited cellars, which are so numerous in our great cities. In these dark, damp, unventilated caverns, fevers, consumption, and rheumatism reign unchecked. Here, thousands are born only to die. Compared with many of these, the Irish squatter's extempore shanty on the outskirts, is a palace of health and luxury. Surely, Humanity and Law ought long since to have combined (as they did in Liverpool), in shutting up for ever these underground dens of disease and death.

More frequently the class of persons especially in view, are found occupying apartments in buildings erected for the purpose, or converted to it from other uses. The ground on which they stand was chosen, probably, because it was cheap ; and it was cheap, perhaps, because its air was unwholesome—darkened by the smoke of a gas factory, or made intolerable with the

stench of some slaughter-house, or distillery. In devising such
structures, it would seem as if the owner had but one idea—
namely, that of getting the highest possible rent for the least
possible accommodation. Accordingly, the rooms are small,
badly lighted, unventilated, inconvenient, and uncomfortable.
The stairs are narrow, steep, and dangerous. The entrance,
halls, and other parts used by the tenants in common, are too
often insufficient in space and ill-arranged. It is easy to see
what are the natural tendencies and almost inevitable conse-
quences of living in such a place. What is everybody's business
is nobody's. The portions used in common are neglected, and
become filthy. Bad habits soon prove themselves progressive
and contagious. Even the neat housewife, when surrounded
constantly by dirt and disorder which she cannot remove nor
control, gradually loses her ambition and sinks to the surrounding level. In such close proximity to neighbors, there can be
no feeling of privacy, no security from intrusion. The bounds
which should shut in and preserve the family are overrun and
obliterated. No selection of companions can be made for
children, however unfit and demoralizing the associations to
which they are condemned. Parental restraint soon loses its
hold, and frequent quarrels among both parents and children,
result from an intercourse so compulsory yet so intimate. The
latter, growing up amid such scenes, can never know the
attractions of home. The former lose, ere long, their domestic
tastes and feelings. Debarred from exercising those finer sympathies and affections which mark a well-ordered family, the
whole household soon learn to find their pleasures in low and
rude excitements, if they do not fall, as is but too likely, into
intemperance and open vice.

It is true, indeed, that there are in all our cities many leased tenements which are not obnoxious to the above objections ;—houses, single, or in blocks, where more or less of isolation and privacy, and family comfort may be had. In reference to these, however, and to all other hired habitations, there is another important point to be considered—namely, that of expense. Ask the great army of tenants of every grade, what item in their expenditure seems heaviest and is met with the greatest reluctance, and most will say, *" the rent."* And yet it is not they who pay the largest sums that have the most reason to complain. The man who hires a whole house can generally suit himself, and usually obtains an abode by paying the average rates. With the poor it is not so. In this matter, emphatically, their destruction is their poverty. It is a well-known fact, that no houses yield so high a profit to the landlord as those which he rents to persons who can least afford to pay. Against such exactions, so long as this class continue to hire their habitations, there is no help. It is the penalty imposed upon them for their inability or their unwillingness to be their *own tenants.* It would be well for such persons to enter into a little calculation. It is not difficult to prove that what they now pay for poor lodgings, would soon procure for them a decent house of their own, and give their families the precious boon of a permanent home. And what a comfort, to fear no more the quarterly or monthly returns of rent-day, and to be for ever freed from the cost and damage of compulsory and frequent removals ! If well selected, the little property will be likely to rise in value, and can hardly fail to constitute the beginning and the nucleus of other acquisitions.

While he is a tenant, the man must take such a house or

room as he can get, not such as he needs. As purchaser, or builder, he may adapt his dwelling to the wants and circumstances of his family. As a tenant, he suffered a thousand inconveniences and mortifications rather than to make improvements on another man's property. Now he can have his habitation repaired, painted, and kept in good condition, without asking consent of a niggardly landlord.

If the benefits of such a home ended here, how fully would its acquirement justify many sacrifices, and the most strenuous efforts. It is the moral influence likely to flow from such a change that suggests the highest motives for attempting it. To have a home which he has himself reared, or purchased,—a home which he has improved, or beautified,—a home, indeed, which, with honest pride and natural love, he calls *his own*, is an additional security for any man's virtue. Such a home he leaves with regret ; to it he gladly returns. There he finds innocent and satisfying pleasures. There his wife and little ones are happy and safe,—and there all his best affections take root and grow. To such a pair, as time advances, this abode of their early and their middle life, this hive where their offspring once swarmed, and whence they have perhaps all departed, becomes constantly more dear ; for it is now a scene of precious memories,—the undisturbed shelter of their declining years. And say—what lapse of time, what travelled distance, what varied experience of prosperity or sorrow, can ever efface the good impression made by such a home on the tender heart of childhood ? To the tempted youth, to the wanderer from virtue, to the sad victim of misfortune, such a remembrance has often proved a strengthening monitor, or a healing balm. Nor can this kindly influence wholly fail, so long as the dear objects of that familiar scene retain a place in memory, connected as they inseparably are, with thoughts of a father's counsels, a mother's tenderness, a sister's purity, and a brother's love.

CHAPTER III.

HOME IN THE COUNTRY.

 UT it may be said, that this talk about possession and permanency is all very well for such as have the means to buy or to build, but is only a tantalizing mockery to those who with difficulty raise even the monthly payments for their landlords. We do not, however, admit the impeachment. We would be the last to excite expectations which cannot be realized. We will endeavor to show that our views and objects are not only practical but practicable. We address, especially, those who experience and feel the evils of hired abodes in populous places. We assure them that their case is not hopeless ; but we do not say that the desired change can be effected without effort, or without some sacrifice. Few things in life worth having can be got except by resolution, industry, and self-denial. Listen, then, while we try to convince you that the object recommended is an attainable one, and that its benefits will repay all their cost and a great deal more.

First, then, we do not counsel you to buy or to build within
city bounds. Not but that possession, even here, is far better
than tenancy at will. It is enough now to say that the high
value of city lots, their limitations in regard to the style of
building and its material, and the rates of taxation, put such
ownership out of the question for most of you. Happily the day
is forever gone, when the necessity of being near their place of
labor or business, compelled all the work-people and tradesmen
of a city to live within it. Steamboats and railroads, convey-
ances both rapid and cheap, have brought the once distant hills
and fields and groves, as it were, to our very doors. The ines-
timable privilege of a country home can no longer be monopolized by the wealthy citizen. We wish to show that it may
be, and should be yours.

It is well known that at the distance of a few miles, and of
less than one hour from the heart of every great town, building
ground may be obtained at prices which bring it within the
reach of all but the poorest. The organization of village associations has made it practicable for a man with little capital or
credit, to secure a homestead in a good neighborhood. This is
accomplished by means of small but regular payments. Each
instalment reduces the principal, and soon the purchaser is an
owner in fee simple. Do you not see how easy the change is?
That the money which you are now paying in quarterly rent
for an unhealthy and uncomfortable tenement, will suffice, in
two or three years, to give you a good house and garden in the
country? This is not fancy but fact, as figures prove—a blessed
fact, if you will but test it.

It is true that you and your family will be called to relin-
quish some associations and friendships, some privileges, (at

first,) of church and school, some amusements, perhaps, that
you have learned to relish in city life. But mark what compensation ! You gain a *home*—that which you never truly had
nor can have in the hired city lodging. A HOME ! We
might leave it there, for the word comprehends all that is most
to be prized in life. Instead of a house, built only to be let,
and to yield profits to its owner, you have, or should have, one
made for your own accommodation and suited to the condition
and uses of your family ; a house which the pleasure and pride
of possession will prompt you constantly to improve and adorn ;
a house not squeezed in between others, not dimly lighted in
front and rear, not looking out upon pavements and brick walls,
but standing by itself, surrounded and, (when you so choose,)
permeated by the free, pure air, with a grass-plot on which
your children can play, with flowers and shrubs, and shade-trees
and fruit-trees of your own planting, and berries and vegetables
of your own raising. What suitable and comfortable abodes
can be thus secured at a very moderate outlay will hereafter be
shown, with details and estimates of actual cost.

It is clear that in such a residence the expense of living
may be sensibly diminished, while its actual comforts will be
largely increased. Such a family should produce, in part, at
least, their own vegetables, poultry, eggs, and pork. In very
many cases, a cow might be added, and this single advantage
would more than pay if the trouble of living out of the city
were ten times what it is. Think of the difference between re-
galing your little ones on pure, nutritious milk, and poisoning
them with a compound made from the vile leavings of the distillery ! Nor is it only in the supplies of the table, that the
country life would prove less expensive. In matters of dress,

furniture, &c., the tyrant fashion which lords it over all classes, would be somewhat less exacting there.

Add now what would be gained in point of health. The amount of disease and mortality among city children is absolutely appalling. Even in our healthiest summers, the deaths during the hot months are often doubled, and the new victims are drawn almost entirely from the ranks of childhood. Can it be doubted that a large part of these might be saved, if sent to the country and cared for there ? Fond parents, carry thither your own, and see how soon their sallow cheeks will glow with ruddy health, and their soft emaciated muscles round into firmness and strength and beauty.

But rural life can claim other and still higher praise. Its moral influences are as much better than those of the city, as its air is more salubrious. Experience seems to say that in the country, only, can *men* be reared. From it the leech-like city receives ever new recruits, while itself produces almost none. To the country we must look as the proper home and nursery of children. Here they are away from the dangers and temptations, the unnatural excitements and morbid stimulants, the thousand baits and haunts of vice, with which the city abounds. Here parental authority is less counteracted, family discipline is more easily maintained, and the virtues, affections, and benefits of home are more frequently and more effectually secured.

On this agreeable theme, the peculiar and beneficial influences of rural life, it would be easy and pleasant to expatiate. One or two additional hints must suffice.

So far as material objects exert an influence on the mind and heart, the advantage is almost wholly in favor of the country. In the city, every thing is subject to change. Few, comparatively, own their homes, and even they can seldom connect them with the thought of permanence. There is little within them, there is nothing at all around them, about which memory and affection contrive to twine their invisible, but indestructible threads. For the dweller in town, Nature can hardly be said to have an existence. True, the blue heaven bends over his head, but he seldom sees it except in streaks and patches. He must climb high if he would behold the magnificence of its fretted vault, and look upon the sun as he rises or goes down in kingly state. In the country alone can earth and sky be seen in all their beauty and grandeur. Its favored dwellers may not always or fully appreciate these qualities, but they do not therefore escape their influence. The rugged mountain and the gentle eminence, the lake, the river, and the brook, the forest and the grove, the broad plain and the little green dell, must make deep and lasting marks on the minds of those who daily behold them, and especially of those who grow up among them. It is eminently amid such scenes, as history and observation show, that the hardy and homebred virtues thrive, and that patriotism is born and nurtured.

In the country the abodes and occupations of men are more widely separated than in dense communities, so that their life and labors are more often solitary and silent. Such a condition is evidently conducive to thoughtful habits. Among such men we look for frequent instances of marked individuality in character. They are not all moulded into one form by the surrounding pressure. Their sharp corners are not worn off by attrition with the crowd. Not moving in masses, they have opinions and feelings and perhaps prejudices of their own. There may be some evils in this, but there are advantages also. They may seem less courteous, but are they not more sincere? Among them we look for plain good sense and sturdy independence. Above all, their moral and religious convictions are of a higher tone, and are obeyed with a strength and tenacity of purpose, which we seldom find in any class of city population.

This trait of individuality suggests not only a plea for country life, but an important consideration for the architect. Let him remember and consult it when planning for rural homes. Let them be in some sense emblematical of their self-relying occupants, suited to their condition, and not out of harmony with their taste and character.

To men familiar with city noise and activity, the quiet country often seems sluggish and monotonous. Unhappy they who have become unable to appreciate the power and beauty of repose! Be assured that in these calm scenes may be found a peace and joy unknown to the restless town. In the culture of domestic affections; in training your children to habits of industry, learning, and goodness; in reading and reflection; in the pleasant toils of the garden; in social intercourse with your neighbors, and in good offices to all who need them,—you will find healthful and delightful occupation for every hour which you are permitted to pass at home.

This is not an imaginary picture. The experiment has been tried by thousands, who are now enjoying its fruits; by men, women, and children, who once wilted and pined amid stones and bricks in the close city air, but who now luxuriate among trees and grass and flowers, and feasting upon their own unbought dainties, are happier than kings.

CHAPTER IV.

THE VILLAGE.

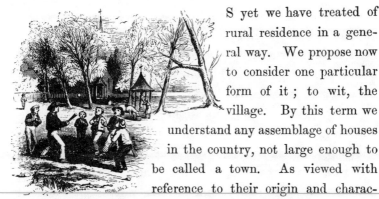

S yet we have treated of rural residence in a general way. We propose now to consider one particular form of it ; to wit, the village. By this term we understand any assemblage of houses in the country, not large enough to be called a town. As viewed with reference to their origin and characteristics, American villages may be divided into three classes. Of these, by far the most numerous are those which have grown up gradually, and naturally, round certain central nuclei. A court-house, a meeting-house, a head of river navigation, a waterfall, a landing, or a railroad terminus, are among the seminal points from which such villages spring. In the second class we place those which have been created by manufacturing enterprise. Thirdly, we have the suburban village, a comparatively recent invention to relieve the hard-working and severely pressed population of our cities. As appropriate to our general object, and with the hope of calling attention to a matter that has been too much neglected, we offer a few remarks and suggestions on the laying out and building of villages.

In villages of the class first named, we find, as we might expect, great variety. They have grown up, not according to any original purpose or plan, but as the increase of business and population demanded. Their appearance is modified not only by the character and occupations of the inhabitants, but by the nature of the site, and the original laying out of roads and lots. If the ground be uneven and the streets irregular, the village must exhibit similar traits. Nor is this want of uniformity and exactness, in itself, objectionable. Many old villages, with their short, and winding, and often narrow streets, have a picturesqueness and ever-pleasing variety, which we are sorry to miss in those that have been laid out by rule.

When places of this class are in their incipient state, a few influential persons may often do much toward giving a right direction to their future growth. The main thoroughfares will, of course, be first built upon. We cannot bring ourselves to feel that such avenues should all run in straight lines, and cross at right angles. This is supposed to be the unfortunate necessity of cities, where every square inch is measured and has its value. In the country, where there is room enough and to spare, there is no need of this mathematical economy. Here the natural way is generally the best way. The character of the surface, making it easy to run a street in one direction, and not so in another, may very properly determine its location. Sometimes this will depend on the eligibility of building sites, or on the accidents of water, of hill and plain, of marsh and ravine. Such requirements will not be wholly disregarded if taste and judgment have a voice in the matter. Nature must be humored and not forced, if we would retain her power to please.

As such villages increase, the districts appropriated to dwelling-houses should receive particular care. The first object should be to make the building lots ample, convenient, and pleasant, and then let the street conform. This principle is to be observed with proper modifications, but its importance will be conceded by many who have witnessed the ill effects of a course directly the reverse. The reservation for public use and enjoyment of some open space in every village, cannot be too strongly urged. The triangular points formed by roads that converge at acute angles, may well be made open ground, instead of being covered with unsightly wedges of wood or brick. Looks and comfort will be promoted by placing the church and the school-house at some little distance from the noisy and dusty street.

In those hamlets, usually of slow formation, which grow up in agricultural towns, many of the villagers—sometimes the larger part—are, more or less, engaged in farming operations. This fact naturally influences (as it ought to influence), the style of building and the general aspect of the place. The new houses, though designed in some respects for different uses, ought not to be wholly out of harmony with the old—nor is there any reason why men should be in haste to get rid of the early old-fashioned farm-house, which, however little it may boast of artistic grace, is yet pleasantly suggestive of rustic plenty and comfort, of manly independence, and of the home-born virtues. From a disregard of such considerations, some of our inland villages are disfigured by the most absurd and incongruous architecture.

Without further detail, where much might be said, we pass to the manufacturing village. This is usually the creation of a proprietor, or of a corporation. Simultaneously with the erection of a mill, tenements are put up near it for the accommodation of its operatives. When the establishment is large, a little town is thus built, as it were, in a day. Such opportunities seem peculiarly favorable for introducing good specimens and models of village and cottage architecture. It is not often, however, that we are able to praise them, either for the taste which they evince or the practical wisdom. Frequently these tenements are long, uniform blocks, built like rows of small city houses, and with equal frugality of space. Far too often they occupy unsheltered and unpleasant sites, without the slightest air of comfort or neatness, much less of beauty. We might urge upon the philanthropic proprietor his unquestionable obligation to make the abodes of his work people comfortable and agreeable. On him who would be considered not devoid of taste, we might press the duty of gratifying, or certainly of not offending the public eye. But there is another appeal which all understand. The pecuniary interest of the proprietor is promoted when he furnishes pleasant homes to those who are in his employ. If the original cost should be somewhat greater, it will be far more than repaid in the long run. It secures in the first place a more intelligent and respectable class of operatives,—people who have been accustomed to the comfort and independence of a home, and who will not go where they can have neither the reality nor the semblance. Such habitations do much towards substituting a permanent for a shifting population. Other and stronger ties are formed than those which depend on mere wages. The pleasant rooms, with their associations of domestic and social enjoyment ; the little garden with its fruits ; the small green yard, with tree, shrub, vine, and flower, which the occupants have planted, tended, and learned to love, are so many pledges of fidelity to their employer. Such homes will not be lightly abandoned with the first fancied or real difficulty that may occur.

It will at once be seen that these remarks do not apply to long blocks of houses. In some respects single tenements, with more or less of open space around them, would undoubtedly best favor the ends suggested. Nearly the same results may however be obtained by having two habitations under one roof. The economy of this arrangement, both in building the house and in keeping it warm, will generally give it the preference. Each tenement may thus have its own yard, garden, and surroundings. In another part of this work will be found some simple designs for these double houses.

For similar reasons the judicious proprietor will be careful in fixing on the site for his tenements. The nearness of a spot to the mill, its cheapness or want of fitness for other purposes, will not be deemed sufficient reasons for putting human dwellings on it. So far as may be practicable, let considerations of salubrity and pleasantness, of soil, and sun, and air, of shelter and of prospect, have their due share in the selection.

It is almost needless to add that the desired work would be only half accomplished, unless the same regard for neatness, order, and comfort, shall also be exhibited in the mills and their appointments, in the canals and bridges, the walks and grounds.

The third class we have called the suburban village. Like that just treated of it is a sudden creation, the result of im-

perative necessity.   Such villages are springing up in the
neighborhood of our great cities, and already furnish comfortable homes to a large population.   Their desirableness and
utility are unquestionable.   But the selection of their sites and
the style of laying out and building, ought not to be left to
chance, to ignorance, or to the selfishness of speculation.
There is no necessity, as yet, for planting these little towns on
impracticable ledges of rock, nor in or around swamps.   Salubrity of air, abundance and purity of water, pleasantness of
location and prospect, eligibility for building and quality of
soil, are points that should be considered, as well as distance
from the city, and proximity to the track of car or steamboat.

Hitherto the perception and supply of a great and growing
want has been left mostly to landowners and speculators, whose
enterprises in this line could hardly be expected to look very
far beyond the results of "a good operation."   What this
means we all know.   But the object is one which may well
enlist a higher motive.   What more promising field can be
presented to the benevolent man of wealth, who recognizes the
obligations of his stewardship, and wishes that all his invest-
ments should benefit others as well as himself?

Attention has recently been given, especially in England,
to the erection, in cities, of cheap and comfortable houses for
the poorer classes.   These are rented at low rates under reasonable and wholesome restrictions in relation to neatness and
good conduct.   Both in a pecuniary and a moral sense these
noble efforts have proved successful.   Place those who have
been familiar with dirt and wretchedness, where they *can* be
neat, and quiet, and comfortable,—where the lesson of order is
taught by example rather than precept,—where its benefits

are constantly seen and the preservation or loss depends upon their own conduct,—and you bring them under the best if not the only culture of which they are susceptible. By thus accustoming them to respect and help themselves, you prompt the aspiration for better things and make the attainment possible.

All this and more, as we have heretofore urged, applies to the substitution of rural homes for crowded and wretched city abodes. To render practicable such a change, by procuring suitable ground for a city village, by laying it out and providing for its growth, regulation, and future prosperity, on rational, economic, æsthetic, and Christian principles, seems to us one of the most feasible and one of the noblest enterprises in which the philanthropic capitalist can engage. Every dollar thus invested would bring to him not only a satisfactory percentage of interest, but what he would prize infinitely more, rich visible fruits of neatness and thrift, of happiness and virtue. He becomes the founder of a community, beholds with his own eyes the good he has done, and leaves behind him, when he dies, an imperishable monument.*

One thing we may take for granted. Villages of this class will continue to be needed, and through one agency or another

* The attention of the whole country has just been called, (September, 1855,) to a much needed reform, by the announcement of a testamentary bequest, appropriating $50,000, for the erection of model lodging houses for the poorer classes. Should Mr. Lawrence's intentions be judiciously executed, they will prove the beginning of a great movement, for they will show that houses may thus be built, which shall prove alike advantageous to owner and tenant. We regard this, therefore, as the crowning act of a useful and honored life. For while thousands of the sons of science will laud the founder of the school at Cambridge, tens of thousands of laboring men will bless the name of the sagacious philanthropist, who inaugurated a new auspicious era for them and their children.

the want will be met.   No man should venture to give impulse
to such a movement without some sense of the responsibility
which he thereby incurs.   Let him not forget that the health,
happiness, and character of thousands may be influenced for
better, or for worse, by his action in a matter of this kind.   The
selection of the ground and the first direction of the enterprise
rest with those who project it, and accordingly as these are
good or bad, future generations will bless or curse the founder.

In so important an affair as the establishment of a village,
the advice of the landscape-gardener and the architect, and
sometimes also that of the civil engineer, may greatly conduce
to a judicious choice of the site, and to its proper arrangement.
And, as sanitary considerations should have paramount weight,
let medical science, after due inquiry and observation, pronounce
on the salubrity of the spot.   When such precautions shall be
used in the designation of the ground,—when a wise and tasteful care shall be manifest in the laying out of its lots and
streets, in the style and character of the houses and in the
planting of trees, the suburban village will assume a new
aspect.   Then to the eye of the passing traveller it will present
a pleasing, instead of a repulsive picture, while its chief recom-
mendation will be that it offers to those who most need a
home, one that is healthful and inviting as well as moderate in
cost.

We have already expressed our conviction that rural villages
need not and ought not to be laid out with the checker-board
exactness which is supposed to be necessary in cities.   We say
" supposed "—for some good reasons might be given against it
even in these.   On the score both of looks and cost it should certainly be avoided in the country.   By letting the streets follow, in

the main the natural grade, there will be a saving of trouble and expense. The lots upon them will not be spoiled by cuts and embankments. Riding and walking will be facilitated and made more agreeable by the preservation of levels or of easy-climbing graceful curves. It is far more important that the house which is to be your home and that of your family, should be pleasant in its position and surroundings, than that it should be placed at the shortest possible distance from the railroad station,—a distance that will usually be travelled but twice a day. This consideration, duly weighed, will certainly have some influence in deciding how village streets and lanes shall run. From these brief hints on a subject temptingly inviting, we pass to another topic.

The tendency to imitation is perhaps seen in nothing more than in the houses which men build. In all time and every where, this has been more or less the case, but the trait seems to be especially conspicuous in the American mind. The evidence of this is not far to seek. We should have less reason to complain if the disposition to copy would confine itself to forms of real excellence and unquestionable beauty. We can only say "*less* reason," for we should still have some. Sameness, even in beauty, soon tires us. Let the productions of art be

> " Various,
> That the mind of desultory man,
> Studious of change and pleased with novelty,
> May be indulged."

If she must imitate, let her model be Nature, whose infinite variety " age cannot wither nor custom stale."

Unfortunately the copying tendencies to which we now refer

usually run in a very different direction from that of fitness, or of grace. We need not mention instances. To every observant person they are perfectly familiar. Often some peculiarity of material, or form, or ornament, or color, introduced by one ambitious man, sets the fashion for a whole street, or even town. The more uncouth or fantastic or incongruous such features are, the more likely are they to reappear with every new structure that is reared. Surely such mimicry as this is specially unworthy of a people who profess entire freedom and independence of thought and action.

But our subject calls us to notice more in detail certain kinds of imitation to which those who build village houses seem to be prone.

The common farm-house sometimes furnishes the model. We have shown that there are situations where, under proper modifications, this does very well. But there needs no argument to show the folly of building farm-houses in villages which have nothing to do with farming.

Sometimes the house of the farm laborer, or the gardener's, or the porter's lodge, as these are given in English works on cottage architecture, seem to have suggested the design. In the books referred to, these are almost the only specimens given. They meet, probably, the wants of that country, but certainly not those of ours. There, a hovel answers for the laboring man, provided that it seldom forces itself on the notice of his rich employer. But if the poor fellow's constant presence is required at the entrance to the grounds, or in any conspicuous spot upon them, his house must be something pretty to look at. If not picturesque, it will offend the fastidious eye of the master and of his visitors. The accommodation of the humble tenant is but a secondary matter. The state of things among us, as yet, is fortunately, very different. Our working men generally own the soil. They own their houses. They are independent. They *can*, if they choose, live in comfortable abodes, and for the most part, they *do* choose it. The cottage architecture of England was never intended for them, and in putting up their dwellings, they can certainly do far better for themselves and their families, than to copy either the mean or the fanciful structures which the wealthy and proud proprietors of that aristocratic isle furnish to their poor dependents.

To the villager of ampler means, or at least of higher ambition, some neighboring country-seat is apt to hold out its temptations. Architecture and gardening have lavished their graces upon and around it. He is delighted with its looks, and can see no reason why he may not have a villa too, on a smaller scale. When he does this, he certainly forgets the difference between his own circumstances and necessities, on the one hand, and those of his wealthy neighbor on the other. The villa has been built with more reference, probably, to taste than to expense. It may be intended mainly for a summer residence. The indulgence of a large hospitality or some other special purpose may have modified its design; it may or may not be just what its owner wants ; it is hardly possible that it can suit one whose condition is entirely different. Besides, when copied on a reduced scale, it will be quite another thing, and its best qualities may be lost in the change.

More frequently however this imitation of villa architecture is limited to particular features and to ornamental details. If these are transferred without change of form or size to smaller buildings, they do but overload them with superfluous finery. Nor

will the attempt to reduce and adapt them to the new position,
be likely to turn out better. The whole business is bad. It is
simply apish ; a manifest attempt to do something beyond the
builder's power.

Still more senseless is that form of this vice which takes the
city for its pattern. The very features in town houses which
their occupants have adopted from necessity, and to which they
submit as unavoidable evils, are too often copied in the country,
with a servility which is ridiculous. The high cost of ground in
a city compels its inhabitants to live in deep, narrow, lofty
houses, lighted only in front and rear, with some of the rooms
half under ground and others far up in the sky. The man who
has had experience in these matters, who knows the comfort of
basement dining-rooms and basement kitchens, and of deep,
dark parlors and chambers, and who has enjoyed the privilege of
frequent climbing to attic heights, would never repeat the experiment when building in the country.

A country village, content to appear what it really is, is a
pleasant place. It unites the charms of nature with those of
art, and its fairest feature is consistency. But such are not all.
There are some aspiring and silly villages as well as boys and
girls. Certainly those are such, which, despising the rural simplicity that should be their highest pride, vainly endeavor in
their buildings, manners, etc. to imitate the city style. Such
an attempt must be unsuccessful. Some of its faults may be
copied pretty nearly, but the real excellencies of city life are
quite beyond their reach. Of such villages it may truly be
said, that they are neither one thing nor another.

While we alternately laugh at and pity these absurdities
of a vain ambition, we feel only indignant when we see a village

similarly injured through the blindness and the promptings of
avarice. Some man of money has bought a tract of village
ground. It is his purpose to make the most of it. The good
looks and welfare of the village, the interests and wishes of his
neighbors, the health and comfort of those who are to live in
his houses, are of little or no account with him. Taking for
his model some mean block of city tenements, he covers the
ground with narrow cells, and advertises to sell or rent them
as charming rural residences. It would not break our heart to
hear that such a man had been condemned to perpetual in-
carceration in one of his own vile boxes.

One or two additional considerations for those who have
become, or who intend to become dwellers in a suburban village,
are respectfully tendered. And first, they should remember
that the village is and ought to be a distinct and peculiar kind
of society. If wise, they will lay aside those notions, prejudices, and habits, formed elsewhere, which are inconsistent
with their new mode of life. Let them regard the village not
as a little city, nor yet as a mere appendage to some larger one.
It is, or should be, a community by itself, having its own interests, and holding its population together by mutual attach-
ments and dependencies. In common with the more isolated
inhabitant of the country, they can have sufficient ground for a
dwelling, with the luxuries of a garden and an unrestricted
supply of light and air. With the city resident they may
enjoy many conveniences and privileges which can only attend
combined efforts and interests. To specify a few of these.—
Here are good sidewalks, a comfort which he who has lived in
both country and city can well appreciate. Here he has aque-
ducts, or at least wells in common, bringing near him and

cheaply, one prime necessary of life.   Wherever there is a village, there will be shop-keepers, grocers, butchers, mechanics, and it will not long want physicians of all the schools.   Here, too, are supplies for the higher wants of the heart and mind. The opportunities for social intercourse are multiplied.   Reading rooms and lectures are provided.   Schools are maintained, and churches are reared and frequented.

These are important facts.   They are connected with all the details of daily life, and it is for the interest of the suburban village that they should not be disregarded in its architecture.

CHAPTER V.

THE CHOICE OF A LOT.

HEN the building of a house is determined on, the first step to be taken is the selection of a site. This is so important a matter, and has so much to do with success or failure, that it seems entitled to special consideration.

The first question for a man in such case to settle, is that of his needs, both present and prospective. This is not always easy. In making up his list of *may wants* and *must wants*, the future householder will often be as much puzzled as was little Frank, in Miss Edgeworth's charming story. In the case of every man there will be some peculiarities of disposition or of condition which should be taken into the account.

One of the first points to be examined is the relations of the lot to its neighborhood and to other parts of the village. A man doing business in the city, naturally prefers a home near the railroad station or steamer landing. If engaged in some manufactory, store, or workshop, which allows him but scant time for meals, proximity in his home is absolutely necessary. To all such we would say, let this consideration have its due weight and no more. In very many cases, a little shorter or longer walk is of small consequence compared with other things which ought to influence.

The house which is to be a dwelling, only, may stand upon some retired and quiet lane. If it is to be also a place of business, it will demand, probably, a conspicuous location on some frequented street. A social family, accustomed to make and receive evening calls, will avoid much disappointment, inconvenience, and grumbling, by fixing their habitation on a street with good walks. Those who prefer solitude and seclusion, and who like to go to bed early, can generally be accommodated on some by-way, whose rugged path will effectually secure them from visiting bores. For some it is very desirable to be near the church and the school-house, while to others this is a secondary consideration.

Questions of economy are intimately connected with the relative position of the lot, bearing as this does, not only on the first cost and probable rise in value, but also on the expense of building and of living there. It is not every man who can settle for himself such points as these. To understand the present value of property, and the probabilities of its improvement or depression, requires much observation and sagacity. To those who are consciously unequal to the task, we can only say, consult, if you can find him, some wise and disinterested adviser.

But there are some means of judging which are within the reach of all. Such elements of calculation are great thoroughfares, railroads and canals, landings and water-powers; and such, eminently, is the character of a population in regard to energy and public spirit. When these are exhibited, even within a limited range, the effect on property will soon show itself. Thus a single street, with no original advantage over others near it, is sometimes made greatly more valuable through the good taste and liberality of a few occupants. And to make such improvements, fortunately, is not the exclusive privilege of the wealthy and influential. Much may be done by men of moderate means, if there be only an eye for beauty and a generous heart. Humble hands have sometimes planted along the roadside, little elms, or maples, which in after years have given shade and beauty and dignity to a noble avenue, thus adding untold thousands to the value of its adjacent grounds. Wherever such men are found, it will be safe, on speculative principles (and those are our present theme), to cast one's lot among them.

Is the ground favorable for building on? This is a very important point. Excavation upon it may be easy or difficult. It may need much grading, or but little. Its position may either facilitate or impede the transportation of materials. To obtain the needed supply of water may cost little, or it may cost much. From ignorance or inconsiderateness in regard to such matters, many a man has had to spend as much upon his ground alone as he had set apart for the whole cost.

Location will also influence the cost of building by modifying its style and decorations. A house that is secluded and seldom seen, may be simple and plain to a degree which would seem mean in a more conspicuous position.

We might proceed to show in what ways the particular location given to a house, may tend to diminish or to increase the expenses of the family which occupies it, but these will readily suggest themselves to every householder.

In many instances, the neighborhood furnishes the controlling motive that decides where we shall build. We like to live near our relatives and friends, or, at least among our acquaintance. Still more desirable is it to secure proper associates for the young. If the village have a wealthy and fashionable end, there will be some who can live only there. Contiguity to some particular church, or school, or doctor, will have its influence with others. The elective affinities of taste, opinion, and companionship, will always have more or less weight in determining where people shall live.

In a community where all classes are virtually equal, we see no reason why their dwellings should not be intermingled. Let each man select the site that is suited to his wants and taste, and let the house which he puts upon it be such as becomes his station and means. His nearest neighbors may make a greater display. What of that ? If able, they have a right to do so, and if not, they will only be laughed at for their folly. In either case, he will be all the more respected for having shown himself in this respect to be a man of sense. Education and refinement are not confined to any class, and certainly are not monopolized by the rich. Often the most attractive objects in a village are its unassuming cottages, pleasing us by their simple, unborrowed beauty, while more ambitious houses, flaunting in stolen ornaments, are noticed only with disgust.

Besides these questions regarding the relative position of the lot, there are others, scarcely less important, connected with its character when considered by itself. The first of these is its healthfulness. If the air is bad from any cause not to come within the purchaser's control, the defect is vital, and should decide the matter instantly. No other qualities, however valuable, can atone or compensate for this deadly fault.

Next in importance to good air comes an abundant supply of good water. If this element can be brought in pipes from pure and permanent sources, the acquisition is of great value, and will justify the sacrifice, if necessary, of some other comforts. Those who have once enjoyed that unspeakable privilege, an unfailing supply of pure soft water, its unrestricted luxury of washing and bathing, and the comfortable facility which it imparts to many household operations,—may well wonder at the indifference with which this matter is regarded by many. Why, there are hundreds and hundreds of villages in our country, in whose near vicinity are hill springs, or mountain tarns, from which a united effort would easily bring an inexhaustible supply. What folly to be digging deep wells, and daily to labor at clumsy sweeps and wheezing pumps, for a meagre quantity of hard, unwholesome, mineral water, when they might have the soft, pure, sparkling lymph laid on their houses to the very top, flowing perennially for the refreshment of man and beast, and cheaply delighting both eye and ear with the pleasantest of sights and sounds !

And yet how many allow the blessed element to run off and be lost, content to wash in water which turns soap back into grease, and to derange their bowels with muddy draughts from the river, or with solutions of salt and lime from the well. Many regard rain-water as wholly unfit to drink. And so it is when no care is taken to keep or to make it pure. Properly filtered and cooled, it is as palatable as it is wholesome. The cistern may be arranged for this purpose, or the water may be filtered as it is used. A knowledge and right appreciation of this fact make the question of wells less important, and will render some places eligible as building ground, which otherwise would be condemned.

The lay of the land and fitness of the soil for garden purposes, and the raising of vegetables and fruits, will not be overlooked by those who mean to have these pleasant accompaniments of country life.

So far as the exposure of the ground may affect the temperature of the dwelling—whether it shall be high or low, sheltered by hills and trees, or bare and bleak, look toward the sunny South, or at the frozen Bear,—is a matter of feeling, and will be decided one way or another as the enjoyment of summer or of winter is most thought of.

In all that relates to the size, shape, and arrangement of the ground, much must depend on the purposes it is designed to answer. If poultry, or swine, or cows, or horses are to be kept on the place, provision should be made for them where they will give the least trouble and offence. If a stable be needed, a lot with rear entrance will make it accessible, and prevent its being disagreeably conspicuous.

The extent of a building lot should often be determined less by the size and character of the house which is to stand on it, than by the probability that it will be properly adorned and preserved. Some men have no taste for lawns, or flowers, or shrubbery. All they want is a house to live in. They know perfectly well that the ground around it will receive no care from them. The less there is to reproach them for neglect, to offend their neighbor's eyes, and to injure by mere squalidness the surrounding property, certainly the better.

Ample ground, when properly cared for, undoubtedly adds to the beauty and value of the house, and under different circumstances it may detract from both. Without attempting to prescribe the proper relation between the size of houses and of the grounds which surround them, it may be said without much question, that no village lot should be less than fifty feet in front, by one hundred and fifty, to two hundred deep.

In most cases, the style of the house to be erected should be considered in reference to its location. A low, modest-looking cottage, set in some bold conspicuous position,—a structure all stiff, regular, and square, standing on an uneven, oddly shaped lot, are examples of inconsistency and absurdity which almost any person may appreciate. That the house may conform to its location, and the location to its house, let the same principle govern in the selection of the one and the designing of the other ; namely, a thorough adaptation of each to the wants, habits, and character of the future occupants.

At the risk of seeming to transcend the legitimate scope of our design, we venture to add a word or two on the relations of buildings to surrounding scenery, and our obligations to regard such relations. It is an undeniable fact that a structure, neither unpleasing in itself, nor inconvenient for use, may yet be so placed—so entirely out of harmony with every thing about it— as actually to mar the landscape. Thus it has been said, that amid mountain scenery, houses and other works of art should be of an unassuming character ; that only a subdued look can become them in the midst of a vastness which it is impossible for them to rival, and which but proves the littleness of man, whenever, among such scenes, he attempts any ambitious display. The true admirer of nature will make no such mistake. The majesty which is around and above him, will awe him into meekness, and his modest habitation, nestling among the cliffs, will look as if seeking their protection. The illustration suggests and enforces a principle which should govern those who build in peculiar and picturesque situations.

Again, in selecting a site on which to live, let men follow, in some degree, at least, their instinctive inclinations and natural tastes. While the modest and retiring will be best suited in the lowly vale, let the bold and aspiring spirit plant itself on the hill-top. In many parts of our diversified country, there is wide room for choice in these respects. Villages, indeed, as already remarked, have often been spoiled, by an absurd endeavor to make small cities of them, by cuttings and embankments, levelings and straightenings. But the attempt is not always successful. Nature frequently proves too sturdy for these barbarians and, after all, a good degree of variety still remains.

If he who is about to build either in the village or open country, have an eye for natural beauty, and especially if he would cultivate in his children a taste so pure, let him seek an expanded and pleasing prospect. Why should others enjoy, any more than he, delights that were meant for all? For him no less than for his rich neighbor, hills soar, and river or lake sparkles in the distance. For him, in no unimportant sense, that neighbor plants the orchard, and dresses garden, field and meadow. From his little domain who can prevent his looking out with rapture over that fair expanse? Who will reprove him, if, with a heart attuned to praise and thankfulness, he shall call the delightful scenery "all his own?"

CHAPTER VI.

THE ADOPTION OF A PLAN.

NO building can be constructed properly without a well digested plan. This is seldom thought of by those who build small houses. Some idea, indeed, every man has of the structure which he means to erect. He determines, perhaps, pretty nearly its form and size, leaving the details to be adopted as the work advances. The consequence often is a series of mistakes. Deficiencies, misarrangements, and incongruities, make their appearance usually when it is too late to correct the evil. It seems like an absolute waste of money to spend it in alterations, which a prudent foresight would have made unnecessary. Yet how often is such waste incurred. In building, it greatly contributes to economical and satisfactory results, that the owner should have in his own mind a judicious and well matured plan.

A prudent man, we say, before he begins to build a house, will not only count its cost, but he will get a distinct concep-

tion of what it is to be. Its position, material, size, and form ;
the dimensions, shape, and arrangement of the rooms ; its
halls, stairways, closets, and all that comes under the head of
conveniences ; its doors, windows, chimneys, and fire-places ;
its walls, roofs, and floors ; the combination of its timbers and
the modes of its construction, should all be decisively fixed
and clearly understood. And this is applicable not only to
large and expensive structures, but to those of a far humbler
class, as we trust our work will make more fully to appear.

To develope such a plan, so that it may be made intelligible to those who are to execute it, requires thought and
care. Each part should be closely considered, not only by itself,
but in connection with the rest, that every want may be anticipated, and every difficulty obviated. A design so elaborated
will promote economy, by insuring a closer calculation of the
expenses, and more advantageous bargains for material and
labor. It avoids the hateful cost of alterations, and by a skilful disposal of the apartments precludes waste of stuff and
room. It is not the least advantage of such a plan that it
tends greatly to prevent those disagreements, quarrels, and
lawsuits, which often spring up between the owner on one side,
and contractors and workmen on the other. It is evident also,
that a house thus built must be superior to one begun without
forethought and prosecuted at random. It is hardly possible that
proportion and symmetry, convenience, beauty, and strength
should result from the latter course. Weakness and imperfec-
tion are almost sure to attend the alteration which such a pro-
cedure usually makes necessary. Take for instance, the stairways, an important feature requiring careful thought. When
they are not planned in the outset, it often becomes necessary

to make them uncomfortably narrow, or dangerously steep. The foot obtrudes, perhaps, across doors and passages. The hall below and the head-room above are so contracted as to be almost useless, or the floors are weakened and the house injured by cuttings and alterations, which might all have been avoided. Compare any house, thus built, with some well planned dwelling, and the inferiority of the former, both in looks and comfort, cannot fail to appear.

Let every man who proposes to build a house for his own use, consider carefully his particular wants and those of his family in reference to each of the points just now enumerated. Each family has its peculiarities of taste, habits, or condition, which should be thought of and provided for. No house-plan will be likely to meet these, unless they have been anticipated in its formation.

Such a study of the wants and conditions of the household, and of the arrangements in the dwelling which will best secure them, would be a profitable exercise for any man, and might sometimes suggest valuable improvements in the domestic economy.

Let us now consider some of the principles which should govern in the adoption and development of a suitable plan. These are clearly to be found in the purposes and uses of the proposed structure. Reasons growing out of these should determine not only the general design, but each particular feature. The proper inquiry in every case is, not how has this thing been done elsewhere, or by others, but how can we best meet the demands of the present case? And this involves the very important idea of *adaptation*. In the right adjustment of the parts to each other, and of the whole to its main purpose and appropriate conditions, lies the foundation of architectural excellence. Every building is erected for some purpose ; let that purpose, if possible, appear in the structure. Every building is meant to be used ; let its fitness for that use be manifest. Without this qualification it can have neither true value nor real beauty.

Another quality which should pervade every design is truthfulness. Falsehood in words spoken and written, falsehood in human conduct, meets with universal reprobation. Why should it be more venial when perpetrated in wood, brick, or stone, in paint or plaster? We do not mean to ascribe the same moral turpitude to the builder who attempts to deceive the public eye with false shows, as to the deliberate liar in word and action. But we do affirm that such practice is a species of dishonest and unworthy artifice, inconsistent with true Christian integrity, of unwholesome tendency, and as incompatible with the simplicity of good taste as it is with that of sound morals. Of the ways in which these great obligations may be and often have been disregarded, we shall have occasion to treat more particularly when we come to details.

With these leading ideas well fixed in his mind, no one, in designing a cottage residence, need trouble himself much about what are called the orders of architecture. He has some important points to settle before he begins to talk of Greek or Gothic, Elizabethan or Italian. Let us consider for a moment what the case requires.

"Houses," says Bacon, "are built to live in, not to look at." Were this truth uppermost in the thoughts of every man who builds a house for himself or others, our domestic architecture would be greatly modified. It would certainly be more comfortable. Can we doubt that it would be better looking ?

The house which is built " to look at " is very apt to be inconvenient, and if so, it is just as surely ugly ; for apart from actual and manifest utility in a dwelling-house, there can be no such thing as beauty. Shelter from sun and storm, protection against the extremes of heat and cold, the due admission of light and air, suitable rooms to live and sleep in, receptacles for clothing, utensils, food and fuel, conveniences for cooking, washing, and all other labors of the household, together with an ample and convenient supply of good water, may be set down as necessary requisites of every human dwelling. These provisions may be few, small, and plain, or numerous, large, and elaborate, according as the wants, means, and tastes of families vary ; but there is not an item of the enumeration which the humblest habitation, that deserves to be called a house, can afford to spare or needs to omit. In arranging the apartments, special attention should be given to the saving of needless labor and to the promotion of neatness and order. Let the rooms which will be most used, be most closely and conveniently connected. Let the best, the most accessible, and most agreeable rooms of the house, whether below or above, be fitted and kept for daily family use. This has not always been done,—but does it not commend itself to common sense ? Let there be at least one room on the first floor, provided with the means of warmth and ventilation, which may be used as a sleeping-room for age and sickness. The stairs should generally be central in position ; they should always be safe for children, and broad and low for the sake of the infirm and the old. The size, form, and arrangement of halls and passages, have much to do with both looks and comfort ; and the same may be said of the position and character of the chimneys and windows. In placing the rooms which are most to be used, regard should be had to their exposure to sun and air at different seasons. The most absurd mistakes are often made for the want of this forethought. We have seen large expensive houses, whose snug winter parlors looked out upon the north-star, and whose large summer drawing-rooms in the southern corner, basked all day in the sun. Porches, verandahs, window-canopies, etc., if judiciously disposed for use and not for show, will add much to comfort.

But physical enjoyment should not be the only aim. In building, as in every thing else, the intelligent and rightly disposed man will remember and consult his higher nature, and will try to make his house, however unpretending, a teacher and promoter of virtue, by its evident regard for order, neatness, truth, and beauty.

It is a common, and a very pernicious error, to suppose that beauty in architecture consists, mainly, if not wholly, in something that is extraneous and superadded. There are those who never think of looking for this quality in mere form, in symmetrical proportions, or in the fitness of things. In building, they settle first what they regard as the practical points of shape, size, etc., and then proceed to put on the beauty. The natural result is an excess of ill-selected and ill-placed ornament.

Others seeing little value in mere decorations, and unconscious of the union which may and ought to subsist between utility and beauty, forego all considerations of taste, and rest satisfied with unadorned ugliness. Of the two we rather prefer the latter.

We shall not be understood as rejecting ornament. Used under the promptings and guidance of a refined and severe taste, it must always add largely to pleasing effect. But let it take and keep its own place. It is at best but a secondary consideration. Not so with the beauty of form, of proportions, and of fitness. This is always attainable, always pleasing, and may add its grace to the simplest cottage, no less than to the proudest palace. A home in which these qualities are conspicuous, can hardly fail to be regarded by its inmates with constantly increasing pleasure and affection ; and this is the highest motive for their adoption that can be urged. Nor is the gratification which such structures afford to others to be left out of the account. When a house is to be one of many, as in a village, there is an added obligation to make it conformable and agreeable. On the ground, too, of profit, it is certain that beauty has the advantage of deformity. Money spent, not in useless parts, idle splendor, and meretricious decorations, but in imparting to a house those solid and useful charms to which we have alluded, will seldom fail to augment its market value ; and this is a consideration which almost every one appreciates.

If but a single house in a village be well built and handsome, it acquires at once the pre-eminence in estimation and value. Let the village be made up, in a great measure, of such houses, and its superior reputation and pleasantness will make its building lots and its entire property greatly more salable. In such a community, self-interest, as well as a regard for the good opinion of neighbors, will generally deter a man from putting up a mean dwelling-house.

There is a street in one of our large cities, on which, by agreement of the owners, all the houses were required to stand twenty-five feet from the street-line, and to be of a certain class, as regards style and cost. At first, this restriction somewhat impeded the sale of the property. But fast as the street was built upon, its reputation grew, and its lots now command twice the price of others lying near, and which ought to have been just as valuable.

There have been many cases in which the ultimate worth of property has been greatly enhanced by judicious restrictions in regard to the position, character, and uses of the structures erected upon it. But far more numerous have been the instances of depreciated value from the want of such care. How often have we seen whole streets and districts which have been kept from rising, or have even sunk in the market, in consequence of the mean and unsightly buildings which have been erected in them by the original proprietors, or with their consent. Such buildings will have a correspondent class of occupants. There will congregate, if not a vicious, yet a noisy, careless, and filthy population, who, when not made so, are at least kept so, by the gloomy discomfort of their abodes, and the irresistible influence of example.

The example of one good house is sometimes followed by an improvement in the style and taste of a whole village. On the other hand, an unsightly erection at some prominent point acts as a discouragement to those who would fain improve and beautify the place. Such an enormity is not only a serious annoyance to the eye—it is an invasion of other's rights ; a real trespass on one's neighbors, in the view of equity, certainly, if not of law. How often has the intrusion of such an object actually lowered the value of surrounding property, to an amount far exceeding its own ! An offence against the sense of hearing or of smell is ranked as a nuisance, is amenable to law, and may be abated by its strong arm. We have sometimes felt disposed to ask why the eye should be less favored. Is it not subject to trials just as real and quite as severe ? Why should the noble and delicate faculty of vision be less protected by those who make, and expound, and enforce our laws, than the inferior senses that convey to us the pleasures and pains of odor and of sound ?

In regard to those moral considerations which make neatness and beauty so desirable in the arrangements and architecture of a village, we prefer to use the words, and to urge the high authority of President Dwight :—" There is a kind of symmetry in the thoughts, feelings, and efforts of the human mind. Its taste, intelligence, affections, and conduct, are so intimately related, that no preconcertion can prevent them from being mutually causes and effects. The first thing powerfully operated on, and, in its turn, proportionally operative, is the taste. The perception of beauty and deformity, of refinement and grossness, of decency and vulgarity, of propriety and indecorum, is the first thing which influences man to attempt an escape from a grovelling, brutish character ; a character in which morality is effectually chilled, or absolutely frozen. In most persons, this perception is awakened by what may be called the exterior of society, particularly by the mode of building. Uncouth, mean, ragged, dirty houses, constituting the body of any town, will regularly be accompanied by coarse, grovelling manners. The dress, the furniture, the equipage, the mode of living, and the manners, will all correspond with the appearance of the buildings, and will universally be, in every such case, of a vulgar and debased nature. On the inhabitants of such a town, it will be difficult, if not impossible, to work a conviction, that intelligence is either necessary or useful. Generally, they will regard both learning and science only with contempt. Of morals, except in the coarsest form, and that which has the least influence on the heart, they will scarcely have any apprehensions. The rights enforced by municipal law they may be compelled to respect, and the corresponding duties they may be necessitated to perform ; but the rights and obligations which lie beyond the reach of magistracy, in which the chief duties of morality are found, and from which the chief enjoyments of society spring, will scarcely gain even their passing notice. They may pay their debts, but will neglect almost every thing of value in the education of their children.

"The very fact, that men see good houses built around them, will, more than almost any thing else, awaken in them a sense of superiority in those by whom such houses are inhabited. The same sense is derived, in the same manner, from handsomer dress, furniture, and equipage. The sense of beauty is necessarily accompanied by a perception of the superiority which it possesses over deformity ; and is instinctively felt to confer this superiority on those who can call it their own, over those who cannot. This, I apprehend, is the manner in which coarse society is first started towards improvement ; for no objects, but those which are sensible, can make any considerable impression on coarse minds."

Let it not be said that it is impossible so to build as to please all eyes, and that therefore we may as well forego the attempt entirely. So far as others are concerned, the main object is secured when your work is satisfactory to persons of true intelligence and taste. But we must also remember that taste is a faculty highly susceptible of cultivation. Let each one do what he can to awaken it in those who are indifferent to good looks, and to correct it in those whose notions are wrong. There is a power in true beauty, as in all other truth, which, sooner or later, makes itself felt. Any house destitute of symmetry, and of adaptation to its end,—grotesque in form, and tawdry with ornament, will soon reveal its deformity, when seen in contrast with one of simple elegance, honest in every feature, and reared evidently not so much to be looked at, as to live and be happy in.

Consistency is a quality which, in human character, all understand and value. It should no less mark the human dwelling. This will be the case when in size, form, style, details, and cost, it evidently conforms to the character, position, and means of its owner. It violates this obligation when the requirements of its situation, of climate, of surrounding scenery, and of the neighborhood, are disregarded in particular features, or in the general expression of the design.

"Count the cost before you begin to build," is a maxim of all ages, and the prudence which it enjoins is not without the sanction of lips divine. The question of ability is one which every man must settle for himself, so far as to determine what amount he can expend. How a given sum, and especially a small one, may be most economically and judiciously laid out, is quite another affair, and demands very careful consideration. Let it be remembered, that in building, cheapness is not always true economy. To build without a reasonable regard for strength and durability, merely for the sake of saving, evinces but a short-sighted frugality.

The question of economy is not a simple geometrical problem, as some would have us consider it. It is not difficult to decide what form of structure will give, with the least amount of material, and at the lowest cost of erection, the greatest quantity of cubic space. Leaving out of the question looks and convenience, the rule might do for a temporary barn, which is to hold nothing but hay ; and this is about the extent of its application. Hexagonal cells answer perfectly for the storage of honey, and an eight-sided prism looks well as a crystal, but neither form is suited to the ordinary purposes of a dwelling-house.

We have stated some of the principles which should govern, as we conceive, in the planning of a house. To persons accustomed to observe and reflect we believe that they will commend themselves. To such we hope they may prove serviceable, not by inducing them to dispense with the skill of educated artists, but by showing them their need of it, and how they can best employ it. As this is a point in regard to which considerable ignorance and prejudice prevail, we dwell upon it for a moment. The expense of obtaining a proper plan is the objection with some. The short-sightedness of this view has been shown in the necessity, which it so often involves, of additions and alterations, which cost perhaps far more than an architect's fees, and fail to satisfy after all. But there is another class more difficult to deal with. Many a man, with no experience and little study, fancies that he can build a capital house. Architecture, he contends, is no mystery, and ought not to be monopolized. A mystery it is not, any more than other professions and arts in which it is universally conceded that skill is acquired only by long and careful application, and by frequent practice. Any man of good abilities may understand its principles, and may learn how to apply them, provided that he gives to it the requisite time and attention. If actively engaged in other pursuits, he cannot possibly do this. Nor, unless he means to change his business, and to plan for others as well as himself, would the object be worth the pains it would cost. "The life of man," says Repton, "is not sufficient to excel in all things ; and as 'a little knowledge is a dangerous thing,' so professors of other arts, as well as of medicine, will often find that the most difficult cases are those where the patient has begun by *quacking* himself."

Many houses are planned by common carpenters, who, for the sake of securing the job, frequently offer to make the design without charge. When such persons profess to think lightly of professional designers, and boast the superiority of "practical men," as they modestly claim to be regarded, it must not be forgotten that they have a motive. The merits of the question may be very briefly stated. If you are disposed to copy exactly some other man's house, a carpenter is all you need. We trust you are not so disposed. Houses, as we have shown, should be adapted to the wants of those who occupy them, and these are rarely the same in any two cases. Houses need not and ought not to look just alike. Such sameness is monotonous, tiresome, and, when carried far, becomes absolutely disagreeable.

In designs thus furnished, the beauties of form are not to be looked for. Those details will be selected which are most easy to execute, and not those which are most appropriate. Such a draughtsman may give the simple elevation—the meagre idea of a building, seen directly in front. To know how it will look from other points of view, and to give it the proper expression, requires an acquaintance with perspective laws, as well as with the principles of artistic grouping and of architectural effect. Men engaged in the mechanical labor of erecting and finishing have no need of these qualifications ; they have no opportunity for acquiring them, and seldom, if ever, possess them. In practical carpentry, the main requisite is manual dexterity ; but practical designing is a work of the mind. In either case, he is most truly practical who is most attentive to his own special department. By this we do not mean to underrate the advantages which a designer may derive from an experimental knowledge of the carpenter's business. Some of our best architects began thus. To cultivate their taste, and to master the higher branches of their *art*, they abandoned, of necessity, the manual labor of the *trade*, without losing the valuable knowledge which they had acquired of the laws and feasibilities of mechanical construction. Nor, on the other hand, would we disparage the exercise of taste and ingenuity in mechanical builders. No cultivation of these talents is ever lost. We conclude this topic with a single hint. In the studios of those great sculptors, Crawford and Powers, there are many Italian workers of marble. It is not improbable that some of these "practical mechanics" would undertake, for a consideration far inferior to that demanded by their masters, to conceive and mould a WASHINGTON for some American Capitol.

It is an error to suppose that the architect's aid is needed only by those who erect large and expensive houses. The man who in building is compelled to a close economy has, perhaps, even greater occasion for the best professional advice. The architect who is called to plan such a house, and who would make it suitable and satisfactory, must perform a very important duty before he begins to make a drawing. He certainly cannot adapt his plan to the requirements of his employer, until he has ascertained what those requirements are. But so vague, often, are the notions of men, that this is no easy matter. They need help to understand and define their own ideas and wishes. In such cases, the architect must explain, and question, and suggest, until his client, as well as himself, shall have a definite notion in regard to the size, accommodation, style, and cost of the proposed erection, and of those paramount considerations to which every thing else must conform. In this matter of advising, an honorable architect will feel his moral responsibility ; consulting not so much his own fancy, as the character and true interests of those who are to occupy the dwelling. It will be his aim so to adapt the house to the habits, needs, and circumstances of the family ; so to arrange the whole in respect of economy, consistency, and architectural propriety, that the result shall be not only pleasing at first, but from year to year more and more satisfactory.

To do this requires not only the exercise of a cultivated taste but considerable acquaintance with human nature. Each particular occasion demands special examination and careful thought. It is this part of the architect's duty which raises his profession above what is merely mechanical, or even artistic. This, when honestly and judiciously performed, gives to his services their truest value. In this respect, his labors are less affected by the size and cost of the building than many would suppose. Often, indeed, the necessity of designing for a house of low cost increases his difficulties. The man of abundant means can afford to have ample space for every desired accommodation, without infringing on architectural effect. But, in the small dwelling, where every dollar must be made to tell, it requires close calculation and ingenious contrivance, to secure at once utility and good looks. And this difference in designing the two classes of structures holds in regard to ornamental details. Says an eminent English architect : " I am not ashamed to confess that I have often experienced more difficulty in determining the form and size of a hovel or a park entrance than in arranging the several apartments of a large mansion." It is for these reasons that architects cannot afford to furnish appropriate and careful cottage designs for the same per-centage on the cost as that which would remunerate them for those of more expensive buildings. The consequence is that many feel compelled to forego such aid.

Under such circumstances, the next best course for procuring a house-plan seems to be that which many adopt in regard to their wardrobe. He who thinks he cannot afford to order a coat, finds a tolerable fit among the ready-made and lower priced articles of the store.

A common mode of procuring a design is to take as a model some house already built. This particularly suits those who experience difficulty in understanding architectural drawings, and in forming the conception of an object, not actually before their eyes. To the copying of a pattern house, if one in all respects suitable can be found, there is perhaps no serious objection, except the sameness. But it is often forgotten that the house which exactly suits its present location and occupants, may seem quite out of place in some other situation, and may be wholly unfit for a different kind of family. If, as often happens, an attempt be made to modify it by altering its proportions, by curtailment in one part, or by some incongruous addition in another, the probability is that the good qualities of the original will be mostly lost, while their few remaining traces will only show the deformity of the alterations.

The same caution is applicable to the selection of published designs. Those principles which should direct in the formation of an original design ought also to control in some degree, at least, the choice of a ready-made plan. Each man must decide in his own case what is most suitable for him. The designs in this book are offered in the hope that, while they increase the variety, they will add something to the facility with which such a selection can be made.

Whatever the plan adopted, let it, when once fixed on, be firmly adhered to. Even though it should be found in some slight degree imperfect, attempts to improve it after the work has begun will be more likely to result in injury, loss, and vexation, than in benefit. Those who adopt a published design with the idea of modifying it, should remember that a slight alteration may change its whole character, and destroy its value. Such a change can be safely made only in the same spirit as that which governed in the original formation; and to do it well requires at least equal taste and skill.

CHAPTER VII.

BEFORE we apply the general principles which have been stated, to the selection, or the formation of a design, it is important to know what is the prominent desire of the owner in building, and to what extent it shall control other interests. Thus only can we determine the purpose and situation of the different parts, and their adaptation to one another. To this branch of our subject some allusions have already been made, but it requires more minute consideration. We shall discuss it under separate heads.

ECONOMY.—That a man, for the sake of display, or from any other motive, should go beyond his means in building, is a folly acknowledged by all. But men sometimes err on the other side. A penny-wise and pound-foolish frugality is exhibited in the houses which men build for themselves, as often as any where else. The most valuable properties in a house are underrated. They do not get what they need, nor what they can well afford. If from either of the above causes a man's house be inappropriate to his character and condition, the inconsistency is soon apparent to all, and he must sink somewhat in the estimation of his neighbors.

In all cases where expense must be closely calculated, the multiplying of angles in the walls and roof should be avoided, so far as may consist with the main purpose of the house. Durability, low cost, ease of transportation and of working, should govern in the selection of material; and in order to derive from it the greatest benefit, that material should be worked in the most scientific and skillful manner. When economy is thus made the ruling influence, there should be no attempt to conceal the fact. Such attempts never succeed. How much better to challenge admiration for a happy effort to economize, than to incur the disgrace of having pretended to do something which was beyond your power! Especially bear in mind the fact, that beauty and convenience are not only consistent with economy, but promotive of it, far more frequently than men usually suppose,—provided these qualities are properly sought in the forms of the house itself, rather than in ornaments and appendages.

MATERIALS.—In the choice of materials, as in other things, appropriateness must still govern. Among these, stone in its numerous forms holds, by universal consent, the pre-eminence. Walls of stone, well laid, last for ages, are proof against fire, a protection against both heat and cold, and need no paint, either to preserve or beautify them. Were we treating of costly structures, we should have much to say in regard to the comparative merits of the various stones in use, and of the different ways in which they are prepared and used. But for building such houses as we are now considering, stone is not often employed in our country, nor is it likely to be so employed for a long time to come. Where it exists in abundance, where the cost of quarrying is little or nothing, and that of moving and cutting it is slight, stone may be advantageously employed on buildings of moderate cost. Walls of *rough* stone, such as these structures would have, finished with the simple details which alone become them, are plainly more suitable for the open country than for the village. For a farm-house, which is likely to remain such, a structure of this material seems very suitable, plain as it is, and strong and enduring. But for very small houses, especially if located in a village, we should seldom advise the use of stone. Let the young householder build at first of a cheaper material, and when his improved condition shall justify it, he may rear a mansion of brick or stone.

When *bricks* are made near by, or from any cause, are the material most easily obtained, their use in cheap houses is appropriate. They admit a wider scope of architectural form, with a neater and more elaborate finish, than can be given to structures of unwrought stone. Such piles are less clumsy, and perhaps less cheerless. Bricks are also more easily transported, and more easily laid, than stones are ; and these qualities have not unfrequently commended them to village use. But, except in those parts of our country which are blessed with pale clays, brick walls impose the additional expense of paint. In the country, a red house of any material is an abomination to the eye.

For country buildings of small cost, *wood* is the substance most in use, and so it will be, doubtless, for a good while to come. It has not, indeed, the permanent and substantial air of brick and stone. But this constitutes, in part, its merit. Our young men just starting in life begin with small houses, as they ought. But they do not mean, and do not expect to live in them always. There are few, perhaps, who do not hope to see the time when they shall be able to erect a large and handsome dwelling, for their middle and declining years. And the number is by no means small, whose history proves this to have been no idle dream.

As their humble wood cottages are not meant to be permanent, would it be fitting that they should seem so? Undoubtedly they look flimsy and perishable to the foreigner, who has never seen any walls less solid than brick or stone. His impressions are of small moment. So long as this way of building is congenial to the quick spirit and progressive habits of our countrymen, it is also right and fit.

In the use of wood, no less than of more solid substances, regard should be had to attending circumstances. So far as it is suitable, there is an evident propriety in employing such wood as abounds in the vicinity. It should not only be but *seem* easy of procurement. Let us eschew always the miserable, the unpatriotic feeling, which prizes things, (it may be of inferior value,) merely because they are far fetched.

In size and forms let the same consistency be observed. Massive and projecting timbers, far larger than strength requires become a building reared among forests and remote from saw-mills and lumber-yards : for this reason, if no other, that it would be expensive to make them less.

Considerable attention has been directed of late, to walls of concrete, and their much vaunted cheapness has induced a good many persons to put them up. They consist entirely of mortar, gravel and small stone fragments, laid up in wooden shells or moulds, which are removed as fast as the hardening permits Where lime, sand, and gravel abound, and stone, brick, and

wood are scarce, such walls may save something in the cost.
But there are objections to them.   To build them well requires
more skill than is needed for an ordinary stone wall.   They
have a blank and monotonous aspect, unless disguised to look
like something which they are not, and this is a practice that
we never can commend.   But our chief distrust relates to their
durability.   These walls are no new invention, nor are they of
American origin.   There are instances, undoubtedly, in which
they have stood the test of time.   But there have been many
others, and those in climates far less trying than ours, where
they have proved worthless.   Within our own knowledge,
several structures of this kind, erected in Massachusetts less
than two years ago, have already crumbled to powder.   A fluid
concrete of the right ingredients and rightly compounded, may
undoubtedly acquire the hardness of stone.   But as the experiment, if successful, might not prove economical, and if unsuccessful would be disastrous, the question of trying it should be
carefully weighed.

One rule in regard to all materials we would earnestly in-
sist on.   Let them appear to be what they are.   A taste truly
moral and refined abhors all dishonest imitations in architecture.

If for the sake of looks, or of preservation, walls of wood or
of brick are painted (as often they should be,) let it still be
evident that they are *painted* brick or wood.   If on the whole
it is deemed advisable to plaster on the outside, a rough wall
of brick or stone, let it show as plaster, and not ridiculously
pretend to be ashlar.   But outside stuccoing is a process which
we would never advise.   It has no particular advantages, either
of appearance or protection, even supposing that it could be

made to adhere. But it cannot, at least in a climate like ours. We do not believe that any outside plastering can long withstand our fierce alternations of heat and cold, of moist and dry. Certainly we have never seen a wall, thus treated, from which the coat did not begin, in a few years, to peel off. The only remedy then, is to strip away the whole and renew the application; for an attempt to patch but makes the matter worse. It may be shown that some stuccoed houses among us have actually cost more in the end, than they would have done, if built originally of hewn stone, to say nothing of the vexation they caused the owners. To such, the remark of Lord Mansfield would not seem extravagant, "that had the front of Kenwood been originally covered with Parian marble he should have found it less expensive than stucco."

STYLE.—When we are considering a structure, as a whole, or in its parts, with reference to appearance and expression, rather than mere utility and comfort, a close adherence to right principles of design is peculiarly desirable. Although this will set aside many fanciful forms which are common and fashionable, there is no danger of its producing an unpleasing uniformity. While the surface and scenery of the country exhibit an unbounded diversity, and the condition, character, and tastes of our countrymen are almost as various, our architecture, if properly conformed to these, incurs no danger of tiring by its sameness. The servile copying, on which we have already remarked, and the architectural absurdities put up by eccentric or ambitious persons, which are but too common, indicate an ignorance and indifference in regard to the true principles of taste, not destined, we hope, to last for ever.

The fallacy of supposing that architectural beauty consists

mainly in ornament, the mere accessories of a building, has been already alluded to in passing. Its injurious influence is conspicuous every where. The general form of a house is often determined with strict regard to cost and utility. The ornamental part is left for after consideration, and so much of it is stuck on as the owner thinks he can afford. But beauty of outline and shape should evidently be the first consideration, while the decorative portion, if there be any, should be designed simultaneously and form part and parcel of the whole. Such beauty must be imparted at the outset, if at all. The vice in question exists, it is to be feared, in high quarters, and needs to be reformed at the fountain-head. Let us hope, however, that the case is not quite so bad as the words which follow seem to import. "The fact is, I never met with the architect yet, who did not think ornament meant a thing to be bought in a shop and pinned on, or left off, at architectural toilets, as the fancy seized them, thinking little more than many women do of the other kind of ornament—the only true kind—St. Peter's kind—'not that outward adorning, but the inner of the heart.' I do not mean that architects cannot conceive this better ornament, but they do not understand that it is the ONLY ornament ; that all architectural ornament is this, and nothing but this ; that a noble building never has any extraneous or superfluous ornament ; that all its parts are necessary to its loveliness, and that no single atom of them could be removed without harm to its life. You do not build a temple and then dress it. You create it in its loveliness, and leave it as her maker left Eve. Not unadorned, as I believe, but so well adorned as to need no feather crowns." *

*The Stones of Venice, Vol. I. p. 388. London ed. 1851.

Let it not be supposed that attention to this point would necessarily increase the expense. On the other hand, if timely and judicious, it would often diminish it.

The subject of architectural orders may seem somewhat beyond the aim of this work and of our humble designs. We trust that the little which we may say under this head, will not be found inappropriate or useless. Much money has been wasted in this country, and great inconvenience has been incurred, through mistaken notions and idle fancies in regard to architectural styles. Unfortunately, the first impulses of ambition in building took a Greek direction. For a time in the earlier part of this century, it was thought that almost every public structure must be Doric, Ionic, or Corinthian. Accordingly we had Grecian Court-houses, and Custom-houses, Grecian Banks and Churches, Grecian Taverns, and Colleges, and Capitols. Nor was the rage confined to edifices of this description. Both in city and country dwelling houses rose with huge columns at the end, largely consumptive of wood and paint. There is reason to believe that this folly has had its day.

We might urge the weakness of the lintel and architrave as compared with the arch. We might contrast the tame flatness and tiresome sameness of that Grecian horizontal squareness, with the bold, soaring, graceful, and ever varying curves and lines of the best Gothic. We might show up the one, all artificial and mathematically stiff, while the other is easy, accommodating, and full of pleasing analogies that remind us of Nature and its endless diversities of beauty. But it is enough to say here that the Greek construction is not adapted to our wants. It lacks the essential element of fitness to the purposes for which our buildings are erected. Nor is this strange. The temples of Greece, which we absurdly try to copy, were reared not to be used but to be gazed at. They were costly offerings, splendid monuments, set up in honor of some god or goddess, and as evidences not only of individual or national *piety*, but also of wealth, taste, and power. The dark cell of the Parthenon might be employed on some great festival to burn a victim in. For this it answered well enough. Its real use was to help sustain the roof, and to form a central core for the splendid peristyle. A genuine Greek structure of the Doric type, unless it be meant for a tomb, it is impossible for us to have. In proportion as we approach such a result, it is done with great waste of room, material, and labor, and involves a serious obstruction of air and light. Look at one of these abortive imitations. The space below the columns is almost wholly useless. If it be a great public structure, this space is occupied in front by a blank, tedious and sometimes frightful flight of steps. Ecce signum—the New York Custom-House! The huge pillars darken the lower windows and obstruct their prospects. The upper windows are often entirely hid behind the deep entablature, and the occupants of such rooms never get beyond a respectable twilight. This mass of base and colonnade, of entablature and pediment, and of roof to cover them, is very costly, and all the good it does is to make the building difficult of access, and dark, and inconvenient. When these features are of wood, they are still more objectionable, as being not only specially liable to decay, but very attractive and accessible to fire. And finally the low-pitched roofs of this style are wholly unfit to meet the stern necessities of northern climes. If we have dwelt a moment on this theme, it is be-

cause we would aid, in our humble measure, to banish entirely
a style of building which possesses so little of real beauty,
variety, and power, and thus direct the popular mind toward
other modes which combine all these qualities. With the
greatest of modern writers on art, we believe it both desirable
and practicable to educate the people generally in the great
principles of architecture, and thus to create a pure and healthy
public taste. Nor is the subject out of place here if, (as we
firmly think,) he is right in saying, " that all good architecture
rises out of good and simple domestic work ; and that therefore,
before you attempt to build great churches and palaces, you
must build good house doors, and garret windows." For ourselves, we may be pardoned if we add, that these opinions of
the comparative merits of Greek and Gothic, are by no means
new. They were formed in the school of Upjohn, years before
the " Seven Lamps" and the " Stones of Venice" fell like
bombs into the camps of Classical and Renaissance architecture,—and reflection and experience have but confirmed
our faith.

It is not by a servile and ignorant copying of any style, that
our domestic architecture is to be truly and generally improved.
We think it pretty clear in what direction we must look for
any real and great reform, but in seeking it there is need of
caution and judgment, as well as of knowledge and skill.

Among the Gothic cottages, so called, which have sprung
up among us, in great numbers of late years, it is not unusual
to see one so excessively Gothic as to look like a caricature.
The roof is broken and squeezed into many narrow gables, and
makes a prodigious display of pinnacles and verge boards. All
ideas of convenience and use were evidently secondary, if indeed

they entered at all into the designer's thoughts. This is the very reverse of the spirit which inspired the oldest and best Gothic, and which must govern still, whenever it is employed aright.

For the same reason it is evidently absurd to imitate in a country home, either ecclesiastical or castellated architecture. We can hardly imagine any thing more puny than a diminutive *American* copy, executed in this ninteenth century, from one of those stern old castles, which were not only proper but necessary in the days of Front de Boeuf.

Not a few in forming or choosing a design, seem to be influenced by a passion for novelty,—the desire of exhibiting something unusual and strange, that shall at least excite wonder if it fail of admiration. It is a poor motive of action at the best, and in such cases is very likely to result in dissatisfaction.

The aspect of a dwelling-house naturally suggests to us some idea in regard to the character and condition of its occupants. There may be, and there ought to be, in the expression of a house something that shall aid us in this matter. It is not a mere fancy, that the spirit and character of the inmates may be made in some measure to appear in the outward expression of the structure. At any rate, when a man's home is grossly inconsistent with his disposition and circumstances, the incongruity is apparent to all.

Let the construction and arrangement of the house have a distinct reference to the employment of its inhabitant. The soiled and weary mechanic, returning at night, will usually prefer a comfortable nook and plain seat by the kitchen fire-place, or cooking-stove, to a sofa in the parlor furnished with carpets, curtains, and mahogany. He would feel out of place—he would be uneasy and unhappy, if compelled to stay long amid the elegancies which surround the man of property and taste. Let such a person consult his inclinations. If it is quite certain that the kitchen, or common living-room, will be the place of his habitual abode, let that room, at least, be spacious, comfortable, and pleasant. Let him consider that his own every-day comfort, and that of his family, are far more important than any impression which may be made on the minds of occasional visitors. In many village and farm-houses, the parlor, so called, is positively superfluous—a locked-up room, kept for company, opened, perhaps, three or four times a year, where the furniture generally gets mouldy, and the air is always musty.

A sensible man will compel others to respect his employment, be it what it may, by the evident and consistent regard which he shows to its conditions. To ape in one's house, or in any thing else, another, whose position is different, is a sort of confession that you despise your own.

The size of a house will modify, to some extent, its form and character. Regularity and variety are more easily attained in large than in small structures. It is very unwise to attempt the reproduction of a large house by a reduced copy. The comparison which is thus forced upon us, is greatly to the disadvantage of the latter.

The nature of the material used should have an influence in determining not only the general form, but the constituent parts. A given design may perhaps be executed in stone, or brick, or wood, but seldom, if ever, will it be equally appropriate for all. Each material has its distinctive character, and as it must impart more or less of the same to the structure, it demands in each case its own particular treatment.

Scenery and position must be taken into the account. Rustic features look well only in the midst of rural simplicity. Architectural elegance should be reserved for cultivated scenes. The Swiss style of cottage originated in the necessities of mountaineers.   Among hills, it shows to advantage its overhanging roofs, its projecting galleries, and sturdy brackets. In a modified form, it may be adapted to many of our rough hill sides. If one is about to build where Nature is wild and grand, he will do wisely to avoid the regularity of shape, the precision and finish, which look well in the village street.

In what degree will your house be conspicuous ? From what points will it be seen ?   What prospects, near or remote, will it command ?   These are questions which, properly considered, must have more or less influence on the character of your design.

Nor can you, in this important matter, disregard considerations of climate.   It is well to remember that you will need both sunshine and shade.   That there are winds to be courted, and winds to be shunned.   That there will be rain storms and hail storms, and snow storms.   That there will be fierce invasions of winter cold and summer heat.   Against these inevitable assaults of the elements, the defences which you provide should be appropriate and sufficient.

CHAPTER VIII.

COTTAGES OF ONE STORY.

THERE is little probability that houses of only one story will ever be looked upon with general favor in a country where almost every one seems anxious to be getting up in the world. To say nothing of other reasons, the fact that a second or third story can be added with nearly the same cost of foundation and roof, readily occurs to economical people. But there are cases where economy demands the one-storied house. If the structure must be so small that its other dimensions hardly exceed the proper height of a story, this form is clearly indicated. And this necessity will always exist. Multitudes must content themselves with the small, low cottage. Fortunately, it is not without its recommendations. The rooms are on a level. The indoors work is more easily done. There is no toilsome climbing up stairs, nor can children break their necks by falling down them, or from chamber windows. When the wants and means of the owner shall justify it, a wing can be added, or a story interposed.

In places exposed to violent winds, and also under the covert of some sheltering ridge, or grove, a low house is often the most suitable. On large country-seats, the farm-house and the laborer's cottage will generally be made low, that they may not obstruct the view, or become too prominent in the landscape.

In all houses of this sort, there should be special precaution against a damp and impure atmosphere. They should be set well up from the ground, with care to prevent water from settling under, or around them. To avoid breathing the moist and dangerous night air, which hovers near the earth, let each sleeping apartment be ventilated by a pipe, opening at the top of the dwelling, and drawing its supply from above.

DESIGN I.

It is our endeavor here to present an arrangement with the smallest amount of accommodation that seems consistent with a decent and orderly management of the household. It is, of course, fitted only for a family of the smallest size and most moderate aims.

Its apartments are a living-room, L. R., to answer the general purposes of kitchen and eating-room ; a sitting-room, S. R., for reading, sewing, and the reception of friends ; and a bedroom, B. R. Connected with the living-room is a closet, and a passage leading to the wood-room, W. R., in the rear. This may be used for the storage of fuel, and large utensils of the house and garden ; and, in summer, for washing clothes, &c. The cellar stairs may go down from this room. The plan shows no fireplaces. The use of stoves is so nearly universal in houses of this class, that there is but little inducement to provide other means for warming or cooking. Accordingly, the chimneys start from the ceilings. In the living-room and sitting-room there are openings for stove-pipes. The chimney-

PLAN.

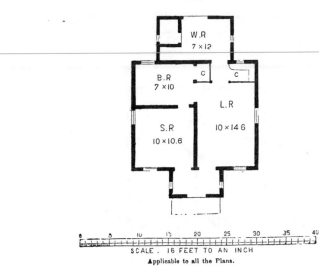

W.R
7 × 12

B.R
7 ×10

C

C

L.R
10 × 14 6

S.R
10 × 10.6

SCALE . 16 FEET TO AN INCH

Applicable to all the Plans.

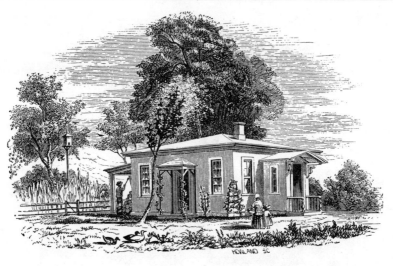

PLAN.

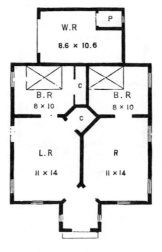

caps are of terra-cotta, and stand on a brick base. The doors are so placed as to make the work and care of the housewife easy, while the sitting-room has all the seclusion that can be desired.

The exterior is equally simple. The wall is covered with vertical boards, and battened at the joints. The window trimmings are plain and cheap, and appropriate to a wooden house like this. These, with the projecting cornice and the entrance porch, make the little structure inviting and homelike, and at once reveal its purpose. To the last-named feature we call attention.

We regard it as essential to a good dwelling-place that it have an entrance-space, or hall, separating the outer door from the rooms in use, and connecting them with one another. The constant occasions of the inmates demand it, and without it there can be no security against the intrusion of unwelcome winds or company.

The projecting gable of the porch, it will be seen, is both a shelter and an ornament.

This house, having but one sleeping apartment, is suited to a married couple without children. Should additional room become necessary, a low second story may easily be added. In such case, the present bedroom might be used for stairway and pantries. With its aspect thus altered, the house would look like Design No. 7, or like No. 9, according to the manner of making the change.

Snugness and modesty are the prominent characteristics of this design. Its most appropriate place would be a small lot in some sheltered position. A neat and simple fence should inclose the ground.

The height of the rooms is 8 ft. 6 in. The cost of the building, as shown, is estimated at $575.

NOTE.—On the tender points of estimate and cost, we are anxious not to mislead. Something of the kind is always expected, and must be furnished. But to do this accurately requires a knowledge of particulars which vary with time and place. Given, the cost of labor and materials at the moment, and on the spot, and a very near approximation can be made. In our estimates we have reckoned nothing for digging, carting, or leveling; nothing for cellar walls, or foundation stone. In many cases, these will involve no outlay of money, while, in most cases, the nature of the ground and other circumstances differ so greatly as to render estimates useless.

As a basis of calculation, we have assumed the following valuation :—

Carpenter's work, at.........................$1 62 per day.
Mason's   "   at.........................$1 75   "
Common labor,   at.........................$1 12   "
Timber and rough boards, at.................$15 00 per M. ft.
Good lumber, at............................$28 .00   "   "
Bricks, common hard, at....................$4 00   "
Nails, at..................................4½ cts. per lb.
Glass, at..................................$2 25 per box.

With the aid of builders of skill and experience, all these designs have been carefully estimated from working plans. We believe that the sum named for each plan is sufficient for its erection in the most perfect manner, at the prices above given. Wherever and whenever the cost of materials and work is either greater or less than we have assumed, the proper allowance must be made.

DESIGN NO. II.

Here we have larger rooms, and four instead of three. A narrow entry opens conveniently into the sitting-room and the living-room,—the corners of these apartments being cut off for the purpose. This irregularity is balanced by the closet in the centre of the house. Without loss of available space, this arrangement is promotive of convenience and good looks. A side-door, opening into the living-room, is protected by an open porch of simple form. By means of light, movable shutters, and a door, this porch in the winter may be changed to a close one. As more suitable to this style of house, a square built brick chimney rises from the ground. A cellar may be made under part of the house, with entrance from the wood-room.

In very small houses we cannot have every convenience. In this, the wood-room does not connect with the interior. If only one of the back rooms be wanted for sleeping, a door may open from the other. The same room will answer for stairs and pantry, should it be found expedient to raise the roof. But this could not be effected so easily as in the former case. This house would form a suitable wing to a larger one erected in front. In this case, the main porch might be carried to the side, the two principal rooms converted into one, and the others used for pantry and store-room.

We have designed this house for a clapboard covering, the horizontal lines of which suit its spreading form and low roof. The details of cornice and windows are very simple, and ornament is scarcely used. The structure is not intended for a prominent point of view, or to be looked at from a distance. It would well become a small regular plot, a little removed from the road, with a neat garden behind it, and open greensward in front ; a fit abode for some aged couple, or widow, where they could still enjoy the independence which they love, and sometimes see their children.

Height of rooms, 9 feet. Cost, about $625.

NOTE.—In explanation of the landscape and foliage shown around these houses, a few words seem proper. It certainly is not intended to offer these accessories of the pictures as models of scenery to be sought, or strictly imitated. This would be generally impossible. They show, at least, what may be accomplished by a judicious disposition of trees, shrubbery, and grounds. They will be useful, suggestively, we hope. To the artists we have endeavored to indicate the general character of the place for which the plan was deemed appropriate. Much was necessarily left to them, and to their taste and skill is mainly due the credit of these pleasing accompaniments. Notwithstanding the opinion of Loudon, we believe that the size and general effect of a building may be better appreciated, amid surroundings like these, than it can be without them.

DESIGN NO. III.

It is needless to say for whom this plan was intended, as the whole family is in sight. The owner, whom you see so busy with hammer and nail, is one of that independent sort, who like to do things in their own way. On the edge of the village he bought a piece of ground, but partly cleared, and which nobody else had thought of. Here, amid the spared trees, he put his house. He wanted but three rooms. You see that they are larger than those of No. 1, and differently disposed. A verandah, where he could sit in the shade, and enjoy the fresh air, he was resolved to have. To carry out his own views of convenience and comfort, he disregarded the advice of neighbors, who insisted that it would be quite as cheap, and much better, to build his house "regular and square." He did nothing for mere fancy. The cornice is unornamented, the front door plain, the window caps are strips of plank sustained by three-cornered blocks. An evident purpose pervades every part of the plan. At first it looked so plain, compared with neighbor-

DESIGN, NO. III.

PLAN.

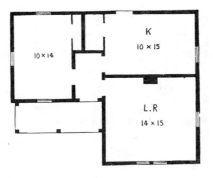

K
10 × 15

10 × 14

L.R
14 × 15

PLAN.

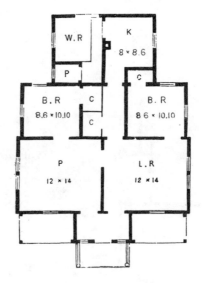

ing houses, which were tricked out in gingerbread finery, that people laughed, and called it barn-like. Not so now. Prairie roses, planted and trained by the owner's own hand, already supply the want of pilaster and cornice. Honeysuckles will soon climb the slender columns of the verandah, and hang between them in fragrant festoons. Ere long, grape-vines will display their purple clusters, where now the bean-poles stand. The maize-patch, at present somewhat too near, will be replaced by grass and flowers; and then, perhaps, some who once scorned the homely dwelling will stop to gaze, and long to enter.

Let them enter. They will find every thing in order within. The interior of the house was planned to suit its mistress. Each room is entered directly from the entry, and this being the only connection between them, no one can be used as a passage way to others. The kitchen, with all its sounds and odors, is effectually separated from the sitting-room. Each of these rooms is supplied with a pantry, and a back-door opens out from the latter. The inside walls are neatly papered. The doors and trimmings are plain and substantial.

Height of rooms, 8 ft. 6 in. Cost, estimated at $650.

DESIGN NO. IV.

This plan combines some of the peculiarities of the first, second, and third. The rooms of the main building are disposed as in No. 2, but, being larger, admit of a passage to the kitchen in the rear. This also allows one of the front rooms to be used as a parlor. The sitting-room, kitchen, and bedrooms have each a pantry.

The exterior, as compared with the preceding, shows more attention to symmetry, and more care in the details. The bracketed cornice, the double verandah, and wide projecting door-hood, bear witness that comfort and taste, as well as cheapness, have determined the choice of style. It would be peculiarly appropriate for a summer cottage, and would answer well for the permanent occupancy of a small family without servants.

Nestling in some sunny nook upon the hill-side, guarded and sheltered by tall old trees, painted of a cheerful color, and decorated with vines and flowers, this cottage would have charms for the dullest eye.

It is not, however, strictly economical. The great extent of roof, as compared with the height, makes the space inclosed more expensive.

Height of rooms, 9 ft. The estimated cost is $1000.

Note.—In all the plans of this chapter, there is an inclosed space between the ceiling and roof. This provision is important, not only to protect the inmates against the heat of the summer sun, but to aid in retaining the warmth of their winter fire. To this space, there should be some mode of access. A scuttle on the rear slope of the roof is probably the best for houses of one story.

CHAPTER IX.

COTTAGES OF ONE STORY AND ATTIC.

A S the structures, called story and a half houses, are usually
built, the roof is low, and the upper rooms, in consequence,
are inconvenient, uncomfortably warm, and poorly ventilated.
With some reason, then, it is asserted that it is better to give
more height to the side walls, and by means of a flat, or very
low-pitched roof, secure a full, though not a high story. It is
conceded that such a story is generally more comfortable than
one in which the ceiling follows the line of the roof. But it
will often happen that *steep* roofs are preferred, and for the best
of reasons, in cases where economy allows only one full story
below them. When this happens, the attic rooms may, by care
in the construction, be made almost as valuable as those with
vertical walls. They can be more easily and perfectly ventilated, and to finish them for use adds but slightly to the expense. We have given more examples of this sort than of any
other, as it must always commend itself to that numerous class
with whom it is an object to obtain considerable house-room at
a very moderate cost.

DESIGN NO. V.

In its general form, this design differs but slightly from many which may be seen in almost every village. Without pretending any originality, it attempts some improvement on a prevalent style of dwelling. It is the smallest size admitting upper-story accommodation.

The two main rooms are separated by front and rear passages, and by the staircase which leads up from the front entry, and is equally accessible to both rooms. The stairs have a platform above the rear entry, from which they are returned over a recess in the living-room, a little lower than the rest of the room. The rear extension may serve as a back kitchen, or wood-room.

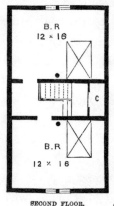

SECOND FLOOR.

A scaffold over the stairs in the second story, which rests on the two cross partitions, sustains the chimney. The recess in the living-room may be inclosed for a pantry. A closet is made on the stair-platform in the second story.

In houses like this, the front door is often near one end, opening into a room. A brick chimney, with a fireplace in each apartment, rises from the ground. The stairs are at the end of the house. The points of difference are manifest, and favor, in our plan, both looks and comfort. No outer door opens into a room. No room is made the passage way to another room. The exterior is regular. The little chimney is an ornament, and the porch invites you and offers its shelter. The form and arrangement of the end windows improve the outside look, while they make the inside cheerful. As this cot-

DESIGN, NO. V.

FIRST STORY.

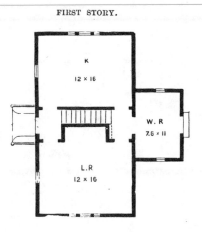

K
12 × 16

W. R
7.6 × 11

L.R
12 × 16

FIRST STORY.

tage is low and would not obstruct the view, it is suitable for a gardener's, or laborer's home, on some large place.   Or it might serve as the temporary abode of some young and growing family, to be made, in time, the wing of a larger house.   In such case it would be wise to place it with reference to the probable enlargement.   The construction and finish of this house are very plain. Its sides may be covered with clapboards, or with vertical boards and battens.

Height of first story 7 ft. 6 in.   Length of posts 11 ft. Cost, $820.

DESIGN NO. VI.

There was a coach-house, no longer needed as such, and the owner concluded to remove it, and convert it into a dwelling. The building was about twenty feet square, with twelve feet posts, and a flat roof.   The plan adopted is shown in this design.

On the lower floor there are two rooms, each fifteen feet long and ten wide,—a good pantry,—two passage ways, and an easy staircase.   The chimney communicates with both rooms.   The cellar stairs are under the others, being lighted by a small rear window.   The rooms, as may be seen, are well lighted. Either room may be used independently of the other, yet not an inch of space or of partition is wasted.

SECOND FLOOR.

The same economy is observed in the second story.

Here are three sleeping rooms, so that this house, small as it is, will accommodate a family of considerable size.

The first story is eight feet six inches high. This leaves two feet six inches (between floor and ceiling) at the side of

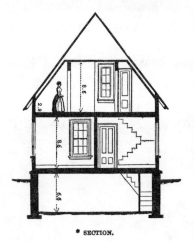

* SECTION.

the chamber. But, two feet from the wall, the height of the room is five and a half feet. This advantage, as the section shows, is due to the sharpness of the roof. As the chambers have a space of nearly eight feet square, where an adult can stand erect, they are evidently but little injured by the slant.

This exterior is also perfectly regular. The side covering is vertical, as better suited to its style. The finish is very plain. The verandah is simply made, with solid posts and brackets. There is a plain shed in the rear. Through a slight error in the engraving, the base of this house does not show as it should. The terra-cotta chimney-caps are simple and cheap.

Height of first story 8 ft. 6 in. Second story 2 ft. 6 in. at the walls and 9 ft. at the ceiling. Cost, $900.

DESIGN NO. VII.

Similar to the last in size of rooms and general arrangement, but more commodious and of higher character. By adding four feet to the length, and by projecting a porch in front, we obtain space for an additional apartment, so that besides the kitchen and living-room, there is a parlor for social occasions. The

* This section is reversed in engraving.

DESIGN, NO. VII.

FIRST STORY.

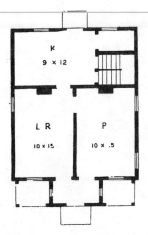

K
9 × 12

L R
10 × 15

P
10 × .5

DESIGN, NO. IX.

kitchen has a large and convenient pantry, and each bedroom is furnished with a closet. Like most of our houses this is designed for a family without servants, and the arrangements of the doors is meant to facilitate the household work.

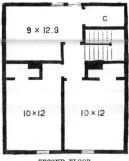

The smoke flues may be carried up as shown, or they may be brought together over the chamber ceiling, resting on the cross partitions, and provided, as in No. 6, with terra-cotta pots. The front windows reach the floor and open like doors, for the better enjoyment of the verandahs. The form of the second story rooms, and the heights of both stories are the same as in No. 6. Cost, $1000.

DESIGN NO. VIII.

Thus far, with one exception, all our fronts have been regular in shape and uniform in parts. In this we have symmetry with variety. The door and window canopies are wholly unlike, and each seems formed as with a single eye to its own utility. But in size, form, and position, they are so proportioned and balanced, so connected by the regular outline of the front, and by the upper windows, stretching partly over both, that there is no feeling of deformity or of one-sidedness in the view.

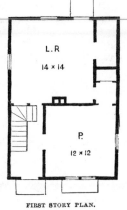

The house has less accommodation than the last. One apartment answers for kitchen and living-room ; but its arrangements are convenient. It has a pantry of gener-

ous size, and communicates directly with the front and rear
entrances, and with that to the cellar; thus saving many steps.
The front window is pleasantly shaded, and has a small balcony,
where roses and geraniums can take the air on sunny days.
The stairs (uninclosed) have a hand-rail, and turn across the

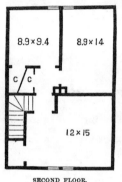

hall at the top, to avoid the roof. On the
upper floor there are three bedrooms and
three closets, the height being the same as in
the preceding two designs.

Numbers 6, 7, and 8 may be classed
together. They will seem appropriately
placed where hills or trees, or other tall objects, harmonizing with their vertical lines,
are seen in connection with them. On a
broad plain, and without shelter, they might
look as if they needed companions.

SECOND FLOOR.

Another suggestion applies equally to the three. The rear
door opens under a plain verandah or shed. Here ought always
to be an inclosed structure, in size and finish suited to the wants
and means of the owner, for the storage of fuel and tools, and for
other useful purposes. Cost of Design 8, $950.

DESIGN NO. IX.

Our plans, thus far, have been formed to meet the wants of
a numerous, but active and earnest class, who are disposed or
compelled to make the most of their means, and who seek considerable accommodation at small cost. The house before us is
of a different stamp. We may suppose its owner to be moderate
in his wishes, and somewhat exact, perhaps, in his habits. With

no family but himself and wife, with a small but regular income, he has built according to his taste and means. No idea of future change or extension entered his head. Its characteristics are simplicity, snugness, neatness and quiet. On the first floor the quiet couple have their pleasant parlor, and their snug little sitting-room, with the kitchen adjoining, and they have two good chambers above. The curved form of the roof, while it makes the attic more commodious, has a substantial and pleasing look. In the cut the floor plan was unintentionally reversed. To restore it, would bring the sitting-room and kitchen on the right of the entrance,

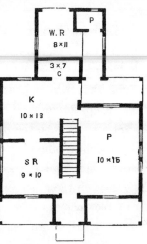

FIRST FLOOR PLAN.

as seen in the perspective. This is easily done, and the same may be done in any other of the plans, should circumstances justify a change of the kind. In an emergency, or by a different family, the small sitting-room may be used as a bedroom. The chimney-top in its character and support is like that of No. 5. The side walls are suited to a vertical covering. The work is all simple and substantial.

SECOND FLOOR PLAN.

Height of each story, 8 feet 6 inches to the ceiling. Second story, 4 feet 6 inches at the walls. Cost, $1,075.

DESIGN NO X.

We have here uniformity of parts without formality, and a good degree of picturesqueness, with convenience of arrangement. The living-room or parlor, occupies the entire front, and is of regular shape throughout. The bay-window, seven feet wide and three deep, improves the outward look, and adds immensely to the pleasantness of the interior. One outer door opens into the hall, which communicates with the parlor, kitchen, and bed-room. This hall contains the stairs, which are not inclosed. The door on the other verandah opens into the kitchen. A lattice screen across the verandah should conceal it from the front. The rear, as shown, has a back-kitchen and chimney, with a

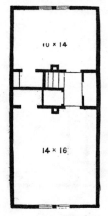

10 x 14

14 x 16

SECOND FLOOR.

wood-room annexed. If not needed, this back-kitchen may be omitted from the plan, a smaller extension for wood-room being substituted in its place. The chimneys are of brick from the ground. The house is well supplied with pantries in both stories. The cellar stairs open from the kitchen. Let the side covering be vertical boards and battens. Clapboards would seriously injure its character. The picture indicates not only the style of the house, but, to some extent, its appropriate surroundings. Let no such cottage stand in a bleak, open field, as if it had been accidentally dropped there, and forgotten.

Height of stories same as in No. 9. Cost, $1,100.

DESIGN, NO. X.

HINLAND. SC.

FIRST STORY PLAN.

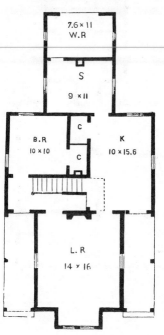

7.6 × 11
W.R

S
9 × 11

C

B.R
10 × 10

K
10 × 15.6

C

L.R
14 × 16

FIRST STORY PLAN.

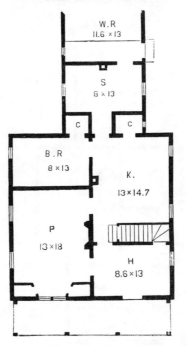

DESIGN NO XI.

This cottage is compact and economical, but with powers of accommodation considerably beyond any of those which have been presented. A good-sized parlor, a comfortable living-room, an entrance hall, large enough to answer as a sitting or an eating-room in summer, and five bedrooms, are comprised within a space of about twenty-seven feet square. A back-kitchen, woodroom, pantries, etc., are furnished in an extension at the rear.

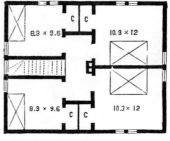

SECOND FLOOR PLAN.

Every room in the house is provided with a closet. In the parlor there are two, so disposed as to give the interesting form of a bay to the front end of the room. Each bedroom has a small gable window, and three of them have a dormer-window each, in addition, of such width as to make them useful and pleasant. The side covering should be vertical, though clapboards will answer.

This house is superior to the preceding ones, not only in size and commodiousness, but in decoration and finish. The roof has a wide projection at the gables, supported by brackets. The dormer-windows have ornamental supporters at the sides, sawn from thick plank, with simple brackets under the cornice. The verandah is ceiled above horizontally. This plan, like the preceding one, is reversed in the engraving. The height of stories the same as No. 9. Cost, $1,500.

DESIGN NO XII.

The house before us, with fewer rooms than its predecessor has, is more costly. But it has advantages, notwithstanding, which will probably commend it to some. Such are, rooms of larger size; a hall which extends through the house (so conducive to summer comfort); the open staircase, with its balustrade; a wider separation of the rooms, and the pleasing irregularity of its external form. A single glance at its features and finish would show to the passing observer, that the owner was both able and willing to consult his tastes as well as his purse.

The arrangement needs some explanation. The stairs, starting just back of the parlor-door, on the right side of the hall, land on a platform, six feet above the floor, from which they re-

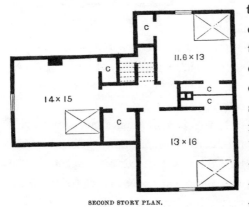

SECOND STORY PLAN.

turn over the bedroom closet. At the rear of the landing, a partition crosses the hall, with a door at the side of the staircase. The cellar flight, starting in the back hall, goes down under the main stairs, that part of it beyond the platform being in-

cased. The back porch is open, and the wood-room is beyond it, with kitchen-pantry, and other conveniences.

In the second story, the stairs land over the partition between the parlor and bedroom. There are two pantries between the

DESIGN, NO. XII.

FIRST STORY PLAN.

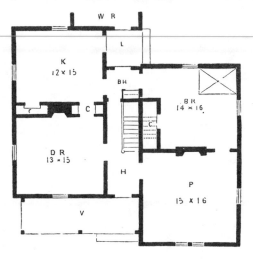

chambers at the right of the hall—one for each. There is a
small one also in the back chamber beyond the stairs. There is
a large closet in the hall for bedding, etc., and a small one in
the left-hand chamber. If needful, this room may be divided
in the centre, and a portion of the hall closet devoted to the
front half. The chimneys are of brick, and topped out with
the same. The small dormer-windows in the roof are intended
for ventilation as much as for light. But they are decorative
features also. The window caps are of plank, supported on
simple brackets. The front gable window has a flower-balcony.
The verandah is solid and plain, and is so finished as to show
its construction. Sawn brackets of solid plank adorn the gable
cornices, while the extended rafters are made to show along the
eaves.

The first story is nine feet high. The second is like those
last described.

Though this house would not be out of place on almost any
village lot, it is especially suited to one somewhat irregular in
surface, or outline. It is well fitted for a corner house, the
fronts, seen in the engraving, showing on the two streets. In
any event, the lot on which it stands should be of good size.

This plan may be easily spoiled. No alteration should be
attempted without good advice. Some practical man may perhaps object to its irregularity. He may wonder that one part
of the house stands back of the other. If he prefer the square,
dreary, double house, so common formerly, and seen sometimes
still, his wish is easily gratified, and for a model he can take a
packing-box.

The cost of this house is $1,625.

CHAPTER. X.

HILL-SIDE COTTAGES.

FROM convenience or from choice, many houses are placed on the hill or mountain side. When judiciously selected and properly built upon, such sites have many advantages. Raised above the miasms which too often float over the lowlands and stagnant waters of the valley, their occupants breathe a purer and more salubrious air. From such points, as from lofty watch-towers, the eye commands, at pleasure, all the variety and beauty of the landscape. Seen from a distance, they are often and should always be points of light and loveliness—such as make us wish we " had wings like a dove," that we might fly away to their leafy shelter and enjoy their cool repose. Notwithstanding the fatigues of climbing and the dangers of descent, the remoteness and seclusion to which such situations are sometimes incident, and their peculiar exposure to the blasts of winter, there are always some who will live nowhere else.

The habitation which is properly fitted to an unusual or rugged site, has a character and beauty of its own. We like to trace in it the evidences of an allegiance to Nature, the confession of her superority. We are pleased to notice what difficulties have been overcome, and to find that such a house can be conformed to its position, and made to harmonize with the scenery, without impairing its usefulness.

By way of calling attention to the advantages which such situations possess, and of suggesting some of the ways in which they may be turned to good account, we offer two designs for hill-side cottages.

Basements, as they are usually made, more or less beneath the surface of the ground, are our aversion. Too often they are damp, almost always ill-ventilated. If city houses *must* have them, they should rank, and generally do rank in the class of necessary *evils*. The man's sanity might almost be doubted who should put a basement to his house in the country. But it often happens that the form of surface and nature of the ground, are such as allow the two sides or ends of a house to be of different depths, thus admitting entrance from without, on two floors. In some families, such a division of the house divides also its duties and labors to great advantage. To give such a story its highest value and avoid the needless use of stairs, it should contain all the rooms and appliances needed for the labor of the household. The apartments should be entirely above ground, well lighted and ventilated. The ground outside should be lower than the floor, and should descend from the house, not only for drainage, but to prevent the settling within of the denser gases and vapors. The floor should be elevated somewhat above the ground, and the side walls should be " furred off " with wooden strips to which the laths are to be nailed, thus forming an air-chamber between the outside stone and the inside plastering. The cellar, back of the rooms, should be separated from them by an air-tight partition, and well ventilated, to prevent the intrusion into the house of its damp or impure air. A due regard to health demands the use of every precaution to secure dryness, to retain warmth, and to exclude those insidious vapors, charged with disease and death, which are wont to gather in dark and low places.

Such a story should be a real story, not a low, mean, back place, but a respectable portion of the house. Let the door be screened if necessary, and let the whole be made pleasing by the judicious disposition of flower and vine, and shrub and tree. Houses thus built cannot easily be regular in form and arrangement. Nor is it desirable that they should be. In placing such a structure, the surface, rather than boundary of the ground, should be consulted. The house must be fitted to the declivity, even though it do not conform exactly to the street.

DESIGN NO. XIII.

This design is intended for a situation higher than the road on which it fronts. Entering at the upper level by a gallery on the side, or by an outside flight of stairs from the front, we come first to a large hall, which may be furnished as a sitting-room, or used, on occasion, as an eating-room. This apartment may be economically warmed by a drum connected with a stove in the room below. The stairs to the upper floor start from this hall near the outer door, and under them is the basement flight, inclosed, with a door at the top. The large bedroom beyond the stairs is provided with a fireplace for use in case of sickness. Connected with these rooms is a smaller bed-room and a good sized parlor. Every apartment on this floor has a prospect in two directions.

PRINCIPAL FLOOR PLAN.

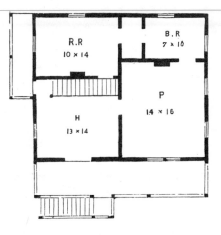

The under story has a large kitchen and a living-room.

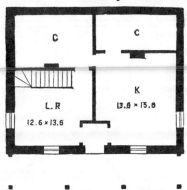

C

C

L. R
12.6 × 13.6

K
13.9 × 15.6

BASEMENT PLAN.

From the latter, stairs lead to the main floor. The living-room is to be warmed by a stove, the flue of which passes under the stairs. There are two cellars which open from the kitchen. In these may be made such pantries as are needed. Make sure of an air-space between the plastering and outer wall, and make small cellar windows in the rear.

The upper floor has two large bedrooms, seven feet high at the side, and four large closets, which are two and a half feet

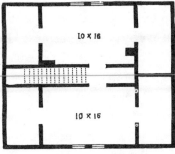

10 × 16

10 × 16

UPPER FLOOR PLAN.

high at the walls. This is owing to the low inclination of the roof. An additional closet may be made opposite the head of the stairs.

This house, with little regularity of detail, has, we trust, nothing distorted or unequal in its aspect. It is designed for a situation where uniformity would involve a sacrifice of utility. Its principal feature is the verandah or gallery covered by the projecting roof, and supported by the open framework. This is at once bold and simple, suggestive of summer enjoyment and of winter protection.

In its main characteristics this house resembles the Swiss cottage. Circumstances similar to those which make this style

proper on the Alpine slopes often exist among us, and it is for
some such position that the design is intended.   It would suit
well the southern side of some steep and rugged hill, and will
look all the better if the grounds around and below it are left
with their natural inequalities, and not tortured into terraces
or graded into tameness.

The construction should be simple and substantial.   The
lower story of rough stone, the rest of wood, and the sides
boarded vertically.   The framework of the galleries and the
eaves should be solid timber, unornamented, and the railings
should be strong and plain rather than nice.   Some native
grape-vine, if the climate allow, might in a few years be
made to spread its shade and fruit over the timbers of the
gallery.

The roof, it will be seen, though not of the steepest pitch,
is still the most prominent feature.   Such it ought to be.
Especially may this be said of all domestic architecture.   In
houses which are low and unadorned, the effect may be obtained
with a slight elevation above, and a moderate projection beyond
the walls.   Higher houses require higher roofs.   Whatever
may be said in favor of the flat roofs on which people sit and
sleep in torrid lands, no such reason holds in our cold and
showery climes.   Here, economy, durability, protection, convenience, comfort, and looks, all petition for a good degree of
height and steepness in the roof.   In regard to this very important point, we ask the attention of the reader to the following remarks of Ruskin.

" The very soul of the cottage—the essence and meaning of
it—are in its roof; it is that mainly wherein conists its shelter ;
that wherein it differs most completely from a cleft in rocks or

bower in woods. It is in its thick impenetrable coverlid of close thatch, that its whole heart and hospitality are concentrated.

"Consider the difference, in sound, of the expressions ' beneath my roof' and 'within my walls.' Consider whether you would be best sheltered, in a shed, with a stout roof sustained on corner posts, or in an inclosure of four walls without a roof at all,—and you will quickly see how important a part of the cottage the roof must always be to the mind as well as to the eye, and how from seeing it, the greatest part of our pleasure must continually arise.

"Now do you suppose that which is so all-important in a cottage can be of small importance in your own dwelling-house ? Do you think that by any splendor of architecture—any height of stories—you can atone for the loss of the aspect of the roof ? It is vain to say you take the roof for granted. You may as well say you take a man's kindness for granted, though he neither looks nor speaks kindly. You may know him to be kind in reality, but you will not like him so well as if he spoke and looked kindly also. And whatever external splendor you may give your houses, you will always feel there is something wanting, unless you see their roofs plainly. And this especially in the North. In Southern architecture the roof is of far less importance ; but here the soul of domestic building is in the largeness and conspicuousness of the protection against the ponderous snow and driving sleet. You may make the façade of the square pile, if the roof be not seen, as handsome as you please, you may cover it with decoration—but there will always be a heartlessness about it, which you will not know how to conquer ; above all, a perpetual difficulty in finishing the wall at top, which will require all kinds of strange inventions in parapets and pinnacles for its decoration, and yet will never look right.

"Now I need not tell you that, as it is desirable, for the sake of the effect upon the mind, that the roof should be visible, so the best and most natural form of roof in the North is that which will render it most visible, namely, the steep gable; the best and most natural, I say, because this form not only throws off snow and rain most completely, and dries fastest, but obtains the greatest interior space within walls of a given height, removes the heat of the sun most effectually from the upper rooms, and affords most space for ventilation." *

The principal story of this house is 9 feet high—Basement, 8 feet. Estimated cost, exclusive of material for basement walls, $1,300.

DESIGN NO. XIV.

Our second hill-side plan is meant for a position below the road. The principal front is therefore on the higher side. Such a situation has usually less of descent and abruptness than those to which the former design is suited. Gentle swells by some valley side, or on the outer margin of a plain, often furnish sites well adapted to this plan. To make it harmonize with such a spot it is broader and lower than the former house. In other respects they are so far similar that the remarks just made in relation to balconies, verandahs, brackets, walls, screens, vines, etc., may be applied equally to this.

* Lectures on Architecture, &c. London, 1854, pp. 34, 35, 36.

DESIGN, NO. XIV.

PRINCIPAL FLOOR PLAN.

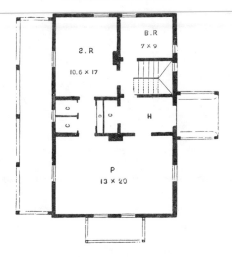

The internal arrangement, as shown by the plans, needs but little explanation. The windows opening on the verandah and on the small balcony at the end, are long and are hung on hinges. The basement has a fuel cellar, F, a vegetable cellar, V, C, a closet, C, and the important rooms L, R, and K. In the attic plan there are four bedrooms and as many closets. These rooms are ten feet high in the highest part, and but two feet and nine inches at the side ; a result which is due to the lower pitched roof. The stairs are of a compact form and occupy but little space. A reference to the section of Design No. 6 on page 80 will show the relation of the upper

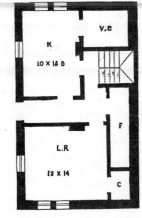

BASEMENT PLAN.

stairs to the roof, and the necessity of some such arrangement as this. The position of the upper flight determines that of the lower, and makes necessary the recess in the stone wall as shown by the basement plan. Where so close a calculation is required, as in this case, a small alteration in one part of a staircase without a corresponding change in some other, may just spoil the whole thing. Indeed few changes in a plan are safe, or likely to be successful, unless they are considered with minute and judicious reference to their bearing on

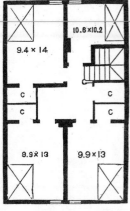

ATTIC PLAN.

every other part ; and this is about equal to original planning

—a thing more easily talked of than done. This point has been alluded to already, but it is so important that we venture to give line upon line.

The position, on the whole, most eligible for this house is one in which its shaded side should face the west, and its parlor windows look out upon the south. The road might wind round its southern end, with a sufficient space between for shrubbery and lawn, while the garden might stretch down toward the vale.

Upright boarding is the proper covering for the sides of this building, though clapboards might be used, if specially preferred. But there are some objections to this once almost universal mode of covering wooden walls, and we may as well state them here.

In the first place, clapboards form a sort of horizontal ruling, and it is a well-known effect of such ruling that it shortens and flattens, to the eye, the surfaces on which it is laid. Now this result is directly the reverse of what is often intended, and should still oftener be aimed at, in architectural designs.

The second objection is connected with questions of light and shade. The strength and character of a building depend almost wholly on the shadows which are thrown upon its surface by projecting members. A structure without projections has no character at all. It is blank and meaningless, just as a human face would be without lips and nose and eyebrows. The horizontal ruling of the clapboards being itself a species of shading, not unlike the parallel lines of an engraving, cannot but weaken the power of the other shadows,—thus impairing, if not neutralizing, this part of the effect intended by projecting eaves, canopies, and sills.

A third objection to clapboards rests on the fact, that when they are used, the trimmings are first attached and the boards then fitted to them. This increases the expense, as well as the chances of imperfect work. The reverse happens with plain boarding. The first cost of thin clapboards is about the same as that of thick upright boarding without battens. In durability and warmth the former is decidedly inferior.

To balance all this the clapboard possesses *one* advantage, and that is the power derived from old habits and early associations. But this power is growing weaker every day.

Height of basement, 7 feet. Main story, 8 feet 6 inches. Cost, as in the last design, $1,375.

CHAPTER XI.

HOUSES OF TWO STORIES.

MANY will prefer the two-story house to any that can be devised in the style to which we have thus far confined ourselves. We may well rejoice that there is so much diversity in the tastes and opinions of mankind, and that this is constitutional. It would be a very uninteresting world if the men of it could, by any means, be brought to build, or to think, just alike.

But the two-story dwelling has important advantages, which make it the best form for a great majority of village houses. The choice between this and a lower style of building should rest on clear grounds. There must be a certain relation between the breadth and the height of a building to give it a satisfactory look of stability. To effect this, the house must cover more ground, and the expense is thus carried beyond the reach of many. We do, indeed, see many high thin houses, and miserable spectacles they are. Sometimes we behold one of respectable proportions, but with a meanly finished exterior,— the resources of the builder not having been sufficient to give him a large house, and a good one too. In such cases, we think it would be well to compromise.

While the low cottage seems modest and retiring, the high,

square built house, has a more forward and assured look. When houses, or men, boldly claim our regards, we have a right to expect that they will give proof of their worth. Such structures clearly need a nice finish, and more of ornament, than those of a less ambitious expression. Look, for example, at Design No. 3. Its rude construction, and simple details, harmonize with the structure, and look well. Put them on a high, conspicuous building, and they would strike the eye as out of place, and mean.

A large house is apt to look blank, cheerless, unsupported, if built without wings, porticoes, or some projecting feature. These, however, if elegant and appropriate, are costly. The designs already presented are of low construction, to bring them within the limits of excellence and cost which we have prescribed for ourselves. The fifteenth and sixteenth designs, which follow, are in style and cost as moderate as we deem consistent with the two-story form. Larger houses might, indeed, be put up for the same cost, but only by the sacrifice, to mere space, of other and better qualities. Such houses, if needed, can be built by any carpenter.

DESIGN NO. XV.

The forms of building that prevail in cities are often copied, or imitated, in the villages which grow up around them. This is natural, though very often unwise. In such places, houses, essentially like the one before us, are very common. In some sense, it may be regarded as a detached member from a city block. We have, however, modified it in some respects.

The kitchen, for instance, has been lifted above ground into the light, and the free air. Standing out, as it does, it helps to neutralize the disproportionate height of the main building. The chimneys which, in the city model, stood by the side wall, are placed next to the hall. This leaves space for windows, economizes warmth, and improves the external appearance, by bringing out their tops nearer the roof centre. The front parlor has a bay-window. The beauty and value of this feature is beginning to be known among us. Many costly houses exhibit it. But it needs not, and must not, be monopolized by the wealthy. Read what Lord Bacon said more than two centuries ago : " For inbowed windows, I hold them of good use, * * * for they be pretty retiring places for conference." And Ruskin thus to the good people of Edinburgh : " You surely must all of you feel and admit the delightfulness of a bow window. I can hardly fancy a room can be perfect without one. Now you have nothing to do but to resolve that every one of your principal rooms shall have a bow window, either large or small." And so, too, Henry Ward Beecher, to the countless readers of the Star Papers : " Our common, small, frequent windows in country dwellings are contemptible. We love rather the generous old English windows, large as the whole side of a room, many-angled, or circular ; but of whatever shape, they should be recessed—glorious nooks of light, the very antitheses of those shady coverts which we search out in forests, in hot summer days. These little chambers of light into which a group may gather, and be both in doors and out of doors at the same time ; where in storms, or in winter, we may have full access to the elements without chill, wet, or exposure—these are the glory of a dwelling."

The frame of this window is carried up to the roof, forming

DESIGN, NO. XV.

FIRST STORY PLAN.

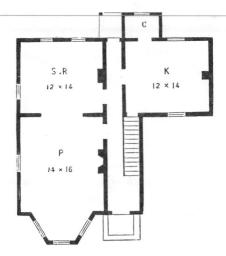

an open balcony in the second story, which communicates with the front chamber. This gives not only a marked feature to the house, but a delightful summer seat.

Back of the main hall there may be an open porch, covered by the roof of a rear building. This should be low and unobtrusive, but well finished. Under the same roof there may be a kitchen pantry. The front entrance is protected by a canopy, in shape adapted to the general style of the house. The main roof is "hipped," that is, it slopes back on every side. A gable is avoided, as it would increase a height already somewhat excessive. Its lowness is partially relieved by a break in the outline,— the part of the roof near the walls being steeper than the rest.

We have shunned what we deem a gross, though very common error in such houses—a large showy cornice in front, while the other sides are left entirely naked. Ours is an honest cornice of real wood ; it is simple and plain, and goes all round. Vertical lines in the covering would increase the apparent height. It should therefore be clapboarded, or better still, planked horizontally with an even surface, showing no joints.

SECOND FLOOR PLAN.

The chimneys are of brick throughout, covered at the top with cement. The posts of the balcony are of solid timber. The casings of corners and windows are plank, and these, if the sides are clapboarded, should be two inches thick.

The foundation walls, above ground, are smoothly laid, whether of stone or brick, projecting, as may be seen, beyond the superstructure, and covered by a wooden base or water-table, which terminates and finishes the side covering. The roof is of tin, laid on an even surface. A gutter is formed in the cornice, which carries the rain water to leader pipes in the rear.

Height of first story, 9 feet. Second story, 8 feet 6 inches. Cost $1,250.

DESIGN NO. XVI.

In exterior form and feature this design has more claim to originality. The rooms, in their general arrangement, are like those of No. 11. There are two large bays on the front, one in the parlor and the other in the hall. The main entrance is at the side of the latter. This is from a porch, partly inclosed by these projections and covered by an overhanging roof.

There are four good chambers on the second floor. Of these three have clothes-presses attached. The front windows of this

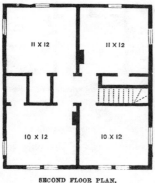

SECOND FLOOR PLAN.

story are double,—two in one. This makes the rooms more valuable, while it gives dignity to the exterior. Many house fronts are spoiled by having too many windows. The wall-veil has no breadth or dignity, and the house becomes a large lantern.

The roof is low and has a bold cornice. The back verandah is plain with solid posts and visible frame-work. There should be a rear building, the roofs joining. In winter, the middle part of the verandah may be inclosed, making an entry to the kitchen and wood-room.

DESIGN, NO. XVI.

FIRST STORY PLAN.

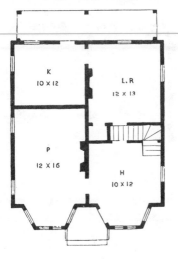

FIRST STORY PLAN.

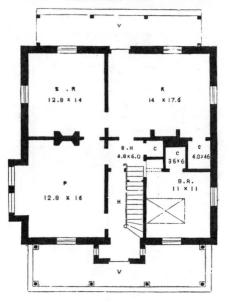

In its general construction and its covering this house is like its predecessor. Its regular form makes it suitable for a spot where it may be seen from several points. The lot on which it is to stand should be open and smooth, rather above than below the grounds about it.

Height of each story, 9 feet. Cost, $1,200.

DESIGN NO. XVII.

A brick house, thirty-three feet square, and finished in the style of this design, can hardly be called a cottage. It is meant to show how the principles which give to humble dwellings a peculiar character, may find application and development in more important structures.

It might be deemed the residence of some individual, happy in his circumstances, temper, and tastes ; of one who knows how to prize the neatness and quiet and comfort of such a home, and who can find in its embellishment a constant pleasure.

The house occupies a level site. Shade trees stand near but do not overshadow it. A deep verandah extends across the front, having in the centre an entrance porch, less deep. The parlor is on the left. Observe its arrangement. Between the doors a piano may stand. On the opposite side is a pleasant bay-window. A cheerful fireplace faces the front windows. Without being stiff or formal, the room is regular, excepting the door at the corner. This is necessary for communication with the adjoining apartment, which may serve as a library and family sitting-room. There is, on the opposite side of the house a bedroom, entered from the back hall. The kitchen, with its pantry and other conveniences, occupies the remaining corner. The stairs have a black walnut rail. Beneath them is the passage to the cellar.

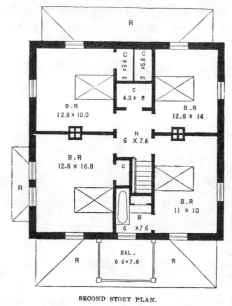

SECOND STORY PLAN.

The upper floor has four bedrooms with closets, and a bath-room, the window of which opens on the front balcony.

The interior finish is designed to show more work than any of the others. The walls are of brick, furred off on the inside with wooden strips to receive the lathing. The form and relative size of the cornice brackets are shown by the cut. The bay window and porch are of brick. The back verandah is plain, the front one more elaborate. The walls and exterior wood-work are painted in colors differing slightly, that there may seem to be no attempt to pass off either material for any thing but what it is.

Each chimney shaft carries four flues, made round and smooth by building them against wooden cylinders, which are raised as the work proceeds. The chimney top may be of cut stone, or cast iron, as one or the other can be most easily procured. This very noticeable feature of every dwelling house is too often neglected. There are thousands of buildings otherwise ambitious and costly, which are meanly surmounted by plain straight heaps of bricks—mere vulgar smoke-pipes. To give it the aspect of stability, the chimney top should have a base where it leaves the roof, and its upper termination should be properly ornamented.   These high conspicuous points should be made to harmonize with the rest of the structure and to enhance the general effect.   They can and they should add grace and dignity to the whole.

The window openings are slightly arched.   They have no projecting caps, but rely for character on the depth of the jambs. In brick and stone work, strength and good looks alike demand the arch.   In wood the case is very different.

This roof is covered with tin, the slope being too slight for shingles.

Height of first story, 9 feet.   Second story, 8 feet.   Cost, $1,875.

CHAPTER XII.

FARM-HOUSES.

MANY of our smaller villages are inhabited mostly by farmers. In others, they are found but here and there, or only perhaps on the outskirts of the busy hamlet. Such husbandmen are not usually of the larger class. Their homes are subject, in some degree, to village influences, and to limitations, from which the isolated and independent farm-house of the open country is exempt. As such, they come within the range of our design. Though the plans given in this chapter are adapted to the village, and its vicinity, it is believed that they will be found not unsuited to the circumstances and wants of many farmers differently situated. We ask attention to their general character and special features.

DESIGN NO. XVIII.

The heart of a farm-house is the kitchen. Around this, all other things must range themselves. The farm has operations and necessities unknown to ordinary households. The demands of hungry laborers must be met promptly and abundantly. These, in busy seasons, come in extra numbers, and are to be provided for in the same kitchen where the ordinary work of the family is done. Besides these, and other labors, incident to farm life, which must often be attended to here, it is usually the eating and sitting room of the household. This multiplication of uses, the good housewife, however she may wish it, can seldom avoid. The number and pressure of her duties, and the small force which she can command for their performance, demands the utmost concentration possible. Accordingly, our kitchen is of generous dimensions. The light enters on two of its sides. There is a large fireplace, which can hold a stove, or range, if desired. The room has immediate connection with every part of the house. Should the house front the west (which is desirable), this room will be in the south-eastern corner. Such an arrangement makes it light and cheerful in the morning, when the work is mostly done, and secures warmth and pleasantness during the winter months. The free circulation of air which is secured by the position of the outside doors will prevent it from being oppressively warm in summer.

In the north-east, and therefore coldest corner of the house, is a large buttery, or store-room, P, connected with the kitchen. Out of this opens a milk-room, D, of good size, with walls of stone. The scullery, or wash-room, S, also leads directly from the kitchen, and has a chimney, with which a boiler, or summer stove, may be connected, if desirable. The outside door of this room opens on a verandah formed by a projection of the roof, beyond the walls of the rear building. Should it be deemed expedient, this additional structure may be extended of the same width, as shown, and without break in the roof, until it connects with the barn. Such an arrangement will furnish a carriage-house, wood-room, tool-house, &c. The verandah, being carried the whole length, provides a dry and neat passage way. Its posts are excellent supports for grape-vines.

It will also be seen that the kitchen connects with a back staircase, which leads to chambers for the hired men, and has cellar stairs beneath; and that besides opening into the parlor, and front hall, it communicates with a bedroom. The last-named apartment can be conveniently used in cases of sickness. The front stairs are open, provided with a railing, and have a closet below for hats and coats.

The parlor, though only second in size, is a pleasant room, nearly regular in its arrangement. There are many families, living in isolated farm-houses, who seldom see, or wish to see company. To them a parlor and front door are but a useless expense and trouble. A room that is rarely opened or aired is scarcely ever fit to stay in. In denser neighborhoods, the case is different. The agricultural family of the village is liable to social·calls, and their occasions can usually be best met by uniting in one the parlor and sitting-room. Such is our arrangement here, and we have aimed to make this apartment the most agreeable one in the house. The front door is meant to be opened, and used daily, and the verandah is for family enjoyment.

Should any occasion bring together in this house a large number of persons, the connection between hall, parlor, kitchen, and bedroom, will permit them all to be occupied.

The second floor affords five chambers. These are five feet high at the walls, and below the ceiling eight and a half feet. The hall is so divided that two of the chambers connect with the back stairs, and the other three with the front flight. If preferred, the door of the central rear chamber may be at the

DESIGN, NO. XVIII.

FIRST STORY PLAN.

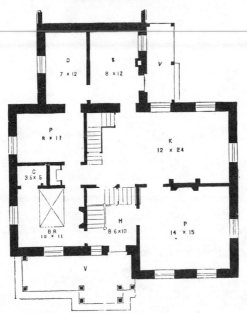

left hand corner, and thus open into the back hall. This room, and that which adjoins it on the right, are lighted by dormer-windows, like that seen in the engraving. Each room has its

closet, and a larger one, B C, opens from the front hall. There is also an inclosed ladder to the roof. Three of the chambers are provided with smoke flues. The supply of bedrooms will not be thought too large by those who know the usual wants of such families.

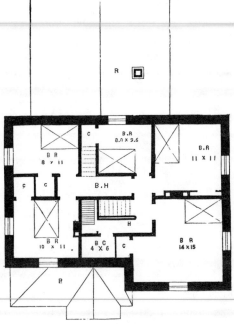

SECOND FLOOR PLAN.

The well-rendered view in the cut, makes unnecessary a minute description of the exterior. The walls are of rough, broken stone, such as many farms readily supply, laid up with all convenient smoothness, but with no outside plastering. The apertures are slightly arched. The trimmings, being almost necessarily of wood, are so formed and disposed as to show their true nature. The posts of the verandah are solid and heavy. The cornice has a framing which is simple, solid, and unique. The sides and gables of the dormer-windows are battened. They would be perhaps better protected, and would look equally well, if covered by shingles, chamfered at the corners.

The expression of this house is consistent with the employment and character (presumed to be alike substantial) of those who are to inhabit it.   It is solid, dignified, comfortable, and individualized.

The first story is 9 feet high.   The second from 5 feet to 8 feet 8 inches.

The cost of the structure would depend very much on the facility of obtaining good stone and lime.   Making no calculation for stone, or cartage, and estimated on the basis named in the note, on page 72, it would be $1,900.

DESIGN NO. XIX.

The convenience of household operations is here combined with a degree of elegance in the better apartments.   The kitchen is connected with the front entrance hall, and also with a short entry, P, leading to a side door, more accessible.   In this plan, some of the heavier housework is transferred from the kitchen to other places.   This arrangement relieves the apartment, and makes it more fit to be a dining and a living room. Its form, dimensions, and position, all favor the same ends. With two windows at each end, it can always secure both air and light.   The fireplace—that all-important feature of a kitchen—is centrally posted on one side.   It is well furnished with closets.   If regularity and symmetry are pleasing, this room must satisfy the most mathematical eye.

Across the entry, P, is the wash-room, containing an oven and a boiler.   From this, a rear door opens into a wood-room. A pantry on the right hand, opening from the kitchen, contains a pump, a sink, and a set of shelves, inclosed.   This also leads

DESIGN, NO. XIX.

FIRST STORY PLAN.

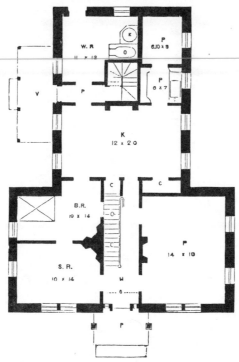

to a larger pantry beyond. The back stairs are ascended from the side entry, and the cellar-way is beneath them. A central hall, containing a straight, open staircase, divides the front portion of the house. On one side is a good-sized parlor; on the other, a snug little sitting-room, and a bedroom of about the same dimensions. All these rooms have fireplaces,—those of the last two being in the corners.

In the rear part of the second floor are two large bedrooms, of irregular shape, each having a closet; and there is also a store-room. Of these rooms, one is lighted by windows in the rear gable, the other by a dormer over the side verandah, not shown in the cut.

Above the front entrance there is a bedroom, with walls five feet, and ceiling nine feet high. The

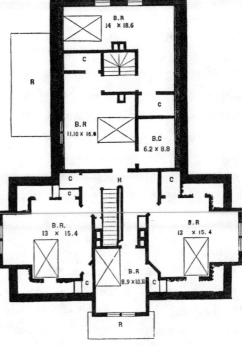

SECOND FLOOR PLAN.

chambers on each side are of equal size, and alike, though somewhat peculiar in form. A space next the walls is inclosed for closet room, so that no part of these chambers is less than six feet high, while they are nine feet in the central portion.

The hall may receive light through glass over the door of the front bedroom.

This is one of the plans whose features can be transposed. That is, the right-hand rooms, in front, or in rear, or in both, may be put on the left, and *vice versa.* The side verandah may be extended to the wood-room.

The construction is meant to be similar to the design last given, but ruder somewhat. Unless stone, which will do without much cutting, can be easily obtained, the lintels of the windows, together with the supports of the projecting gables and cornice, are designed to be of solid oak timber, built into the walls. The gables themselves may be either battened or shingled. In the latter case, much is gained in looks by cutting off the corners of the shingles, but it costs a little more.

The object of this house cannot easily be misapprehended. It tells the whole story in its own honest face.

Height of first story, front part, 9 feet ; rear, 8 feet 6 inches. Cost, estimated as in the last, $2,700.

DESIGN NO XX.

This, in some respects, approaches more nearly than the others, a type of houses often seen. Its second story, at the lowest part, is nearly as high as many that are finished with flat ceilings. It is frank and confident, but still modest, snug, and quiet, as becomes a farm-house. This subdued expression may be ascribed to the descending direction of its principal lines,—to the long declivity of the main roof, which extends over the verandah, and gives the aspect of a lean-to,— to the meek-looking dormer, which peeps out from the centre,

DESIGN, NO. XX.

FIRST FLOOR PLAN.

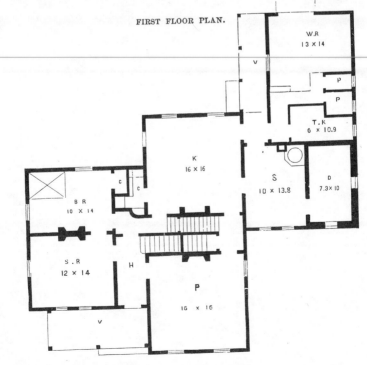

W.R
13 × 14

V

P

P

T.K
6 × 10.9

K
16 × 16

S
10 × 13.8

D
7.3 × 10

B R
10 × 14

C

C

S.R
12 × 14

H

P
16 × 16

V

—to the far projecting eaves, which reduce the apparent height of the side walls,—and to the character of the chimney-tops. Its diversified form (only a part of which is seen in the engraving) will make it a pleasing object from whatever point it is viewed, and will give it a new aspect with every turn.

A single glance at the cut shows this house to be of wood. The windows are of the form most common, trimmed with a casing and band, which project far enough to cast an outline of shadow. The cornice is neat and substantial. The brackets are simple and strong,—meant for support in reality, as well as in appearance. The solid verandah posts are chamfered, with neat brackets at the top.

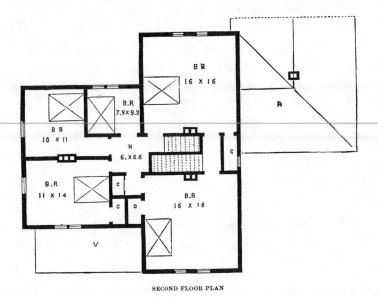

SECOND FLOOR PLAN

In its external finish, this house makes no show of rusticity. It belongs evidently, to a region where saw-mills and planing-machines, and good workmen, are found. It would be no unsuitable companion for our best village edifices.

Its interior arrangements also show an adaptation to the habits and conditions of village life. The front hall communicates on one side with a sitting-room, and on the other with a parlor, and by the principal staircase with the upper floor. Back of these stairs is a lobby, connecting the parlor with the kitchen, and yet separating them. The back stairs rise from this spot, and under them, opening from the back hall, are those to the cellar. A pantry, with interior closet, opens from the kitchen. There is a closet under the front stairs, and the bedroom has one. The facility of communication between all the rooms will not fail to be noticed.

These apartments comprise the first floor of the main building, and in themselves would furnish suitable and sufficient accommodation for almost any village family. The additional room required by the farm economy is provided for by a one-story extension. Here, compactly and conveniently arranged, are the back-kitchen, s., with chimney, and large boiler; the dairy, D., surrounded by hollow walls, for the preservation of an even temperature; a tool-room, T. R., a wood-room, etc. The second story has five sleeping rooms, four of which are provided with smoke flues. There is also a good supply of closets. The smallest of the bedrooms is lighted by a dormer window in the rear roof. All of these rooms may be entered from the upper back hall, and two of them also from the landing of the front stairs.

Height of first story, 9 feet. Height of second story, from 5 feet to 8 feet 6 inches. Cost, $2,450.

CHAPTER XIII.

DOUBLE COTTAGES.

IN cities and villages, two or more families often live in the same house. Numerous and grave objections to this practice readily suggest themselves. To possess the best, the true qualities of a home, each tenement must have its own exclusive grounds, entrance, passages, and stairs, as well as its individual rooms. But where space is limited, and land is dear, and dwellings are brought close together, it is sometimes advantageous to make two distinct habitations under one roof.

When this course is pursued, there is a wider interval between the buildings, than if each house should stand detached on the centre of its own lot. This not only favors the general appearance of the street, but facilitates a tasteful improvement of the ground.

As this arrangement saves not only a part of the material, but all the exterior covering and finish of two entire walls, it is decidedly promotive of economy. As three of the sides are still open to the light and air, the convenience and comfort of the house may be nearly as great as though the tenement stood singly. Sometimes the necessity of having a blank side, or some other unfortunate condition of the building ground may give to this mode a decided preference. In chapter fourth, we have already spoken favorably of these erections, as suited to the necessities of a manufacturing place, and as a desirable compromise between the costlier single tenements and the more economical, but odious block of continuous houses.

In each of the following designs the two houses are precisely alike, constituting in their union an edifice of uniform appearance. We have not attempted by any artifice of construction, to conceal the fact that there are two families here. As a matter of truth, of taste, and of convenience, we think it better that the fact should appear.

Each house should have its own inclosed back yard and vegetable garden. But in front the ground can be more easily and more highly adorned, if the yards are thrown together. If there be a separation, it should be made by something slight, as a fence of chain or wire.

DESIGN NO. XXI.

The body of this building is nearly square. A lean-to is carried round three of its sides. In parts this is left open and forms verandahs, v v. In the inclosed portion we have the entries, E E, and the pantries, s s, adjoining, and the sculleries, with chimneys, in the rear corners. The arrangement of each house is distinctly seen in the plan. The chief entrance is through the side entry, from which point rise the stairs. The cellar stairs are under them and lead from the kitchen. The closet behind the stairs may be made to open from either parlor or kitchen.

There are three chambers on the second floor of each house, well provided with closets. If thought best, the space in the

FIRST STORY PLAN.

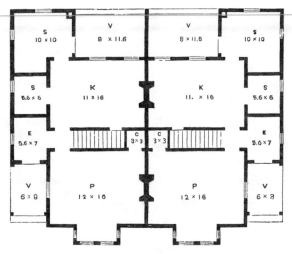

FIRST STORY PLAN.

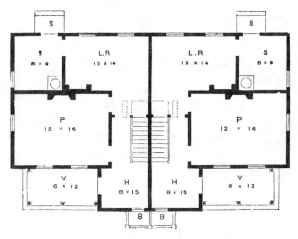

rear of the stairs may be made into one room like that in front. Unless this be done, the back fireplace would probably be needless.

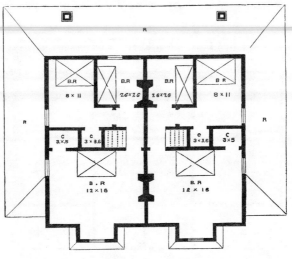

SECOND FLOOR PLAN.

Plainness if not severity marks the exterior. Its sides are clapboarded. Its details are solid, but neither elaborate nor costly. Its principal features are the broad, square bay-windows in front, which being continued up, form the window gables above. These add pleasantness to the house both within and without.

Height of first story, 8 feet 6 inches. Second story, 4 feet to 8 feet 6 inches. Cost, $2,150.

DESIGN NO. XXII.

This building in its general character is similar to the preceding, but somewhat superior to it, as having a larger hall, better stairways, more variety in form of wall and roof, and greater richness of outside decoration.

Nothing in the plan of the first floor needs explanation. The back steps, s, are covered by an open porch, as in Design No. 2.

Each house has four chambers. The small one in the rear

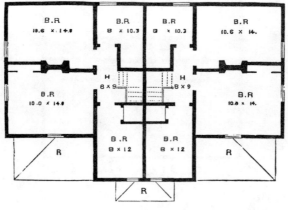

SECOND FLOOR PLAN.

is lighted by a dormer window similar to that in front, though plainer. The closet in the front chamber is raised to give headroom for the stairs. The windows of the front gable are arched, from the necessities of their position, but the variety is not unpleasing.

Height of stories, as in the last.   Cost, $1,950.

DESIGN NO. XXIII.

This is a larger structure, having three rooms on the first floor of the main house. It may be constructed of rough stone,

DESIGN, NO. XXIII.

FIRST STORY PLAN.

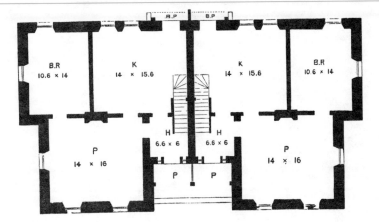

or of brick. The engraving supposes the former. By using bricks, the thickness of the wall would be reduced four inches, and the rooms would be so. far enlarged. The walls, in either case, must be furred on the inside. The window jambs and arches are of brick, projecting beyond the wall. In this design, and only in this one, we have introduced the verge-board. The feature was originally used in Gothic cottages for the protection of a plaster wall, or for the concealment of imperfect work beneath the roof. It was made of heavy oak timber, and outlasted often the walls themselves. The verge-boards of our day are a very different affair. Every body has seen them. Hundreds of cottage gables display the flimsy, steam-sawn, thin board appendages to which we allude. In fact they have become so common, make often so pretentious a display, and are so notoriously unsubstantial, cut-paper-like, and perishable, that we feel some reluctance to use the feature, even when

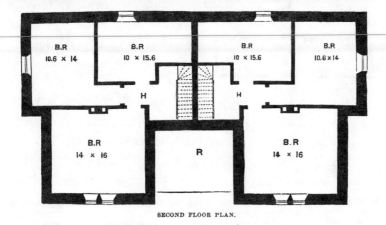

SECOND FLOOR PLAN.

rightly made and appropriately placed. Such details, when employed, should be heavy enough at least to seem serviceable.

In the construction of architectural ornament, so far as it is meant to look like the result of hard work,—the toil more or less skillful of human hands—we believe that resort should seldom if ever be had to labor-saving processes. This would dispense with much ambitious stuff which comes now from the saw-mill and the furnace. But it is better, surely, to do without the decorations, than in them to violate truth and honesty and right principles of art. The verge-board before us is of thick plank, and the cutting aims at simplicity and grace rather than elaborateness.

The interior accommodations of these houses are some-what in advance of the last.

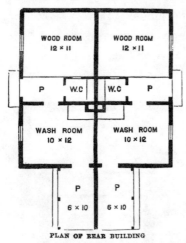

PLAN OF REAR BUILDING

Though more clearly marked as two distinct houses, they are, through the proximity of the front doors, really more social. The rear windows of the second story are dormers like those of the last design. The rear door opens on a back porch leading to a rear building, the arrangement of which is shown in a plan by itself. This is of wood, one story high, vertically boarded and battened.

Height of first story, 9 feet 6 inches. Second story, 4 feet to 8 feet 6 inches. Cost, if built of brick,—main building, $2,525 ; rear building, $475.

DESIGN NO. XXIV.

The objection, already mentioned, to quite small houses of two stories, on the score of looks and proportion, is obviated when they are built in pairs. A suitable relation of breadth to height is thus obtained, and a style of exterior may be adopted conformable to the general outline. The design here presented is an example of this sort. The main building is nearly square, divided through the centre, and containing, in each portion, two rooms, connected by broad doors. These are made in two parts, and may be hung so as to swing back, when opened, against the closet and cellar doors,—or they may slide into the partitions. The side wings, one story high, contain each a bedroom, and a front and rear hall. The foot of the staircase is in the latter,—the lower part being uninclosed. A rear extension, of the same character, contains the kitchens, and their closets, and is made pleasant by verandahs. This may be further extended for wood-room, etc.

The front verandah extends from wing to wing, the central portion being converted into bay-windows, which occupy the entire space from post to wall. These form small apartments of themselves; pleasant recesses, where three or four persons may retire to work, or read, or talk. The opening into the parlor to be finished as the corresponding window, but without sash. A glazed door may be introduced, if needed, in winter. If the parlor be a room regularly used and warmed, these recesses will make convenient and pleasant conservatories. Externally, they relieve the plain surface of the house.

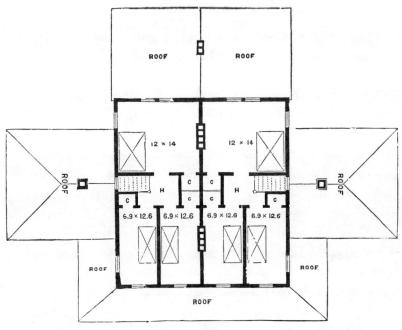

SECOND FLOOR PLAN.

In the upper story, the space in front of the stairs is divided into two rooms, while that in the rear forms one large chamber.

Though this house does not aim at much richness of detail, it suggests the advantages which are derived from mechanical processes, appliances, and skill, and which are fully enjoyed only in, or near large and prosperous communities. The expression thus given makes it a suitable edifice for some large and thriving village. It should be placed on ground elevated a little above the surrounding surface.

Height of each story, 9 feet.   Cost, $3,000.

FIRST STORY PLAN.

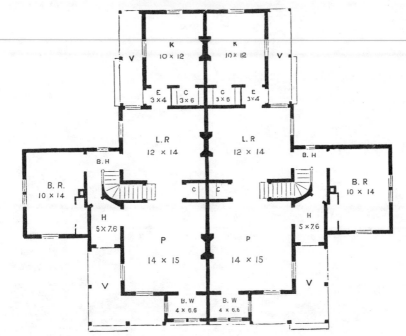

CHAPTER XIV.

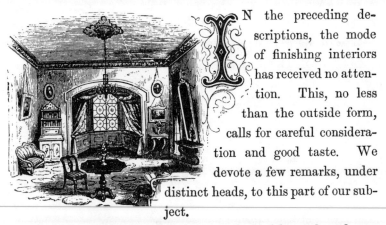

I N the preceding descriptions, the mode of finishing interiors has received no attention. This, no less than the outside form, calls for careful consideration and good taste. We devote a few remarks, under distinct heads, to this part of our subject.

WALLS.—Walls are sometimes covered with wood, and partitions are sometimes made of boards. It is a poor practice, to be justified only by some special necessity. Not to mention other objections, boards are liable to warp, shrink, crack, and let in the cold. All inside walls should, therefore, be lathed and plastered. And as this is a rapid and cheap process, leave no ceiling, from cellar to attic, without a coat of plastering. This will make you safer against fire,—it will promote neatness and good looks,—and, as to the cost, you will soon save it in fuel. To plaster as they do in cities would be, in houses of this sort, a useless expense. The hard, smooth, white finish is not only needless, but undesirable. If the walls are well lathed, a single coat of good plaster, compounded with clean, coarse, light-colored sand, and evenly laid, answers every purpose. It will have a rough sand surface, and will look all the better for it. If you choose, you can give them, with lime-wash, before they harden, some durable color. Almost any light, cheerful tint, is preferable to white. What we have already said respecting deceptive work, makes it almost needless to add, that, under no circumstances, could we approve of marking, or coloring plastered wall in imitation of stone. If something more than a wash be demanded, resort is had to paint, or paper. The former is preferable, as giving a surface that is not injured by water, and may therefore be kept clean. But it is expensive. Paper is easily, rapidly, and cheaply applied, and its use is almost universal. It is not free from objections ; such as the fact that it cannot be washed, is an absorbent of infectious matter, and sometimes harbors vermin. When walls have been several times papered, without removing the former coats, the accumulated layers of paste have themselves become putrescent, breeding fatal disease. For these, and other reasons, we would never paper the walls of kitchens, or of sleeping-rooms. Are not health, and cleanliness, and comfort, a thousand times more important than mere looks ?

In regard to the selection and use of paper, a hint or two may be of service. It is a mistake to suppose that the beauty or fitness of a paper is necessarily proportioned to its cost. If some apartments require a more sober expression than is suitable for others, still let cheerfulness be the prevailing tone. We have occasionally entered rooms where the paper was so dark as to give them an aspect of gloom. In the choice of figures and colors, there is a call for taste. Those pictured walls, however humble their decorations, will play some part in the education of your children. Where there is much blank space, it may be agreeably broken by a decided stripe, or by some prominent figure. In apartments of regular shape, plain papers may be used with good effect, the ground being first laid, and then surrounded with border stripes of a different color in panel fashion. Next the ceiling, a border of contrasting color should always be placed. The tendency of all very large figures, either in wall-paper or carpets, is to reduce the apparent size of the room. All grained and marbled papers, and imitations of stone blocks, mouldings, etc., are so clearly contrary to what we regard as a canon of true art, that we need but name them.

We dislike the custom of papering ceilings. Let these remain so that they can occasionally be brightened and purified with lime.

We have not contemplated having cornices in any of the rooms, unless it be the parlor of No. 17, where a light plaster moulding would be proper.

STAIRS.—The most common, and the greatest fault of stairs, is in making them steep and narrow. This is felt more and more as years advance, and infirmities increase. A low, broad step, is not only the easiest for age, but the safest for child-hood. To secure this great advantage is worth a special effort, and will, if necessary, justify the sacrifice of something else.

In size, and style of finish, the stairways should correspond with the rest of the house. The newell post, hand-rail, and balusters, should be sufficiently large to be actually firm and protective, as well as to look so ; and this is enough for small houses. Where turned work is procurable, it will of course be preferred. Let not those, however, who cannot easily get it, suppose it necessary either to good looks, or good service. Some native wood is preferable to that which is far fetched.

MOULDINGS.—In the use of mouldings round the doors and windows, the same regard to consistency should appear. The trimmings of the smaller and cheaper houses may be plain strips (without mouldings) put on after the walls are plastered. In other cases, the mouldings should be few and simple, neither finically small, nor very heavy. Unless the lines can be well drawn, it is better not to attempt any combination of curves or wave lines. Let each moulding be a single arc.*

Base boards, moulded simply, or chamfered on the upper edge, should project by their whole thickness from the surface of the plastering.

It is poor economy to make the doors of inferior stuff, or so thin that they will probably warp and twist.

PAINTING.—We can apply no other principles to the painting of inside wood-work than those which were stated when treating of exteriors. These require that paint, when used, should acknowledge itself as such, and should eschew all shams. They exclude, of course, the practice of *graining*,—that is, the imitation (by pigments) of wood and stone. This has become so common that we may almost call it a rage. Like other senseless fashions, it will have its day, and pass away. It would be some satisfaction to us could we be instrumental in shortening its reign a single hour.

* In the working drawings of these houses, referred to elsewhere, mouldings are furnished suitable for each design.

What is gained by it ? You admire, it may be, the skill of the grainer. Yet his work can never equal the original, which you might have in its place, and even if it did, the cheat would not be worth the pains. His tints are perhaps pleasant to your eye, and when varnished, wear well and endure to be washed. These are advantages, but they can all be had in plain colors, without the imitation. To copy rosewood or mahogany because you cannot, or will not afford to have the real thing, is mean. To make a false semblance of oak, walnut, or maple, when you might have the genuine article for little if any more than the counterfeit costs, really seems to border on the ridiculous.

But the folly sometimes goes still further. In one of our largest cities there is a public building, whose massive oak dooɪ has actually been painted and grained in imitation of black walnut. Its hard honest face had perhaps begun to look a little weather-beaten, and some citizen painter wanted a job, and so the once noble monarch of the woods must be made to show false colors, and to wear the livery of his former vassal. Some years ago, a small Gothic church was built at one of the fashionable watering-places where oak timber abounds. As a matter of cheapness, the building was ceiled with it. Subsequently, a grainer of the most ordinary kind was employed to paint this ceiling, in imitation of the same wood, and for the modest purpose of making better oak than nature knew how to do. Into such absurdities are men liable to fall when their base of action is not sound. Of kindred origin and character are those mock stone blocks which may be seen even in some costly churches, forming impossible arches, and resting upon nothing, in grave defiance of the first laws of construction and gravity. These practical lies, which are pernicious and offensive every where, are surely most so when they present their brazen hollow fronts in places consecrated to religious worship and instruction.

And now let us ask again, if an imperfect imitation of this or that wood is so pleasing, why not have the wood itself? We have native trees fit for such purposes, in great variety and of much beauty. Besides the harder and more costly kinds, we have pines of all sorts, chestnut, ash, cherry, cedar, maple, mulberry, apple, beach, birch of different sorts, and many more which might in this way be turned to good account. The use of these would impart richness and variety to the inside finish of houses. Oiled or varnished they will retain their natural hues, or will but grow handsomer with age, while the expense and annoyance of frequent painting will be avoided. The light colored woods may sometimes be improved in appearance by a transparent stain, which merely tints without disguising them. Some of these woods will make excellent floors. Why must we always tread on carpets? Our fathers did without them and never complained. For much used rooms they are very objectionable. Dust is constantly absorbed by them, and infection, if it be present, and these pests they are ever ready to give back ; while their own fine woolly particles are always floating above. Let us have some floors so hard as not to need a covering. They should be carefully laid with narrow strips of hard wood, and may be variegated by the alternation of different kinds and colors. They would cost more at first, but as there would be no after expense, except an occasional oiling and rubbing, we think they would prove the cheapest in the end. Assuredly they would, if found conducive to the preservation of health and life.

Window sashes are often made of these woods. In such cases their outside only should be painted. In all cases it would be well to make the strips that secure the sashes, of some hard tough wood, and they should be neatly secured by round-headed screws.

These brief hints might be much extended. We trust they will turn the attention of some who may be about to build, to the applicability and beauty of our common woods, as well as to their advantages on the score of wise economy.

WINDOWS.—Windows are very important and expressive features—the eyes of the house. Their character and effect depend not only on their form, size, and frequency, but in some degree on the style of their drapery and shading.

With a single exception, the bays in these houses are not large enough to be shut off from the rooms. A curtain may supply the place of doors, while each compartment of the window should have its own shade. In some of them it may be well to place permanent seats, such as the carpenter can make, and the frugal housewife can herself cushion and cover.

The coolness and pleasantness of the house are much promoted by suitable window blinds, so fitted that they can be opened and modified at pleasure. Venetian blinds may be hung within or without. If within they are more easily managed, and interfere less with the external appearance of the building. Good finish requires boxes in the jambs to hold such blinds when open. If this be too expensive, let them fold back, one part upon the other, or if the whole window must be open, on the wall.

If wooden blinds cannot be had, all may avail themselves of cloth shades that roll up. These may be linen or cotton, buff-colored or white, the plainer the better. At all events, good friend, when you are about to furnish your windows, do spare yourself the expense of getting, and those who pass by, the pain of seeing, those intolerable daubs called "painted shades," with their preposterous attempts at landscape and architecture, which are now so common in cottage windows.

Curtains are not, like some articles of furniture, absolutely necessary, and very many dispense with them wholly. Yet, in winter, they almost rival the bright fireside in giving to our apartments a warm, cheerful, homelike aspect. If selected with this praiseworthy end, and not for vain ostentation, they will be accommodated to the style of the rooms, and to the means of the family. The window curtains are a fair field for the exercise of housewifely taste and judgment. No need of sending to the city for flimsy gilt cornices. Your carpenter will make better ones of maple or black walnut, and the upholstery part can be done in the family.

KITCHENS.—To insure neatness where it is so desirable, kitchens should be well lighted in every part. The floors especially should be smooth and durable. Stone of large size and even surface makes the best hearth. If brick be used it should be painted.

It is of the utmost importance that sinks should be tight, and that drains which convey away waste water, should be guarded by traps, to prevent the ingress of their foul and sickness-breeding air.

FIREPLACES.—Many of our plans show fireplaces. Others have chimneys without them. These can be retained or omitted at the builder's option. Marble mantels will be deemed beyond the style of these houses, at least for the most part, and no one who has read what precedes, will expect us to advise imitations of marble in any cheaper material. The finish around the fireplace should be plain, and correspondent with the other work of the room, with a firm shelf, supported by suitable brackets.

DOOR-BELL.—Our experience in wear and tear of knuckles

and patience, while we have been knocking for admission at houses in the country, impels us to advise that every cottage have a door-bell. Its cost is small and its convenience great.

ICE.—Ice, once regarded as a luxury, is fast taking its place among the necessaries of housekeeping. Every family should have its ice-box or refrigerator. Its cost is soon repaid in the preservation of meats, etc., and ten times repaid in the comfort it gives. Where the article has not yet come to be one of daily distribution and sale, a number of neighboring families might unite in building and filling a small ice-house.

FURNITURE.—The immediate duties of the architect are performed, when he has completed the house and its apartments. As, however, he is often required to adapt his work to particular articles of predestined furniture, he may, perhaps, be allowed to suggest that the additions subsequently made in the way of decoration and furnishing, ought in their character and expression, to bear some correspondence to his rooms. There are many, and sometimes glaring violations of taste and propriety in this respect. After the architect come the painter, paperer, upholsterer, and cabinet-maker, and these latter often mar, if they do not spoil the best designs of the former. We cannot expect to see consistency and harmony in all the features of our homes, so long as a merely finical fancy, or the selfish interests of artisans and tradesmen, or the absurd demands of ever-changing fashion, are allowed to say how those homes shall be furnished and adorned.

In such matters the future mistress of the house has, or should have a potential voice. Let her be entreated to abjure utterly the folly of imitation. Let her inquiry be, What will best become my circumstances and my apartments? not, How has Mrs. A. or Mrs. B. decorated and furnished hers? Let her remember that simplicity and beauty are kindred qualities. Let it be her special aim to give to her house and to each room, the true homelike air of ease and comfort. Let her remember, that with her it rests whether those rooms shall look stiff, and cold, and repulsive, or shall wear the ever-smiling expression of kindly invitation and cordial welcome. Good sense, good taste, and good morals, alike repudiate the paltry vanity which furnishes a house, not for its constant occupants to use and enjoy, but for occasional visitors to look at and admire.

If these remarks apply to many who build costly mansions, they have a special interest for those whose means are comparatively limited. In trying to be fashionable, none suffer so much as these. Rich people may show but little taste and a great deal of folly in such matters. But the articles which they procure are generally well made, and durable, and more or less comfortable. It is quite otherwise with much of the cheap furniture which is made in imitation, and sold in city shops, and whch is neither comfortable, nor handsome, nor durable. To the young wife or the matron about to occupy her little village home, we would say, be wary of such places. For the most part those mahogany sofas, chairs, bedsteads and bureaus, are mere shams. Like the razor bought by poor Hodge, they are " made to sell." It is vastly better for you to get something less aspiring, but more solid and more useful.

In general it would be well that larger articles should be made specially for the room in which they are to stand. In this way they may not only be fitted to the places they are to occupy, but also to the general character of the house. For cottages of small expense, all that is needed in the way of couches and easy chairs, may be almost wholly of domestic manufacture. The frames, simply but solidly made of some common hard wood, and of convenient form, might be cushioned and covered by the family themselves. In this way much may be done with very small means. We have seen good-looking, home-made chairs, with easy seats and backs, which had been quickly and cheaply manufactured, and with no other frame than a common flour-barrel supplied. Even the hardest and homeliest bench that was ever made of oak plank, is a more comfortable and more respectable article of furniture than many of the spring-seat and hair-cloth sofas and rocking-chairs, which we have met with,—soft, plump, and elastic to all appearance, but which when we, in good faith, accept their invitations, let us down with a sudden jerk, and make us painfully acquainted with their internal mechanism.

In the matter of tables, bureaus, etc., we recommend the same honesty. Let them be of some native wood, solid, and strong and well made. Surely this is better than a perishable patchwork of soft pine, veneering and glue. If you have supplied your best room with well made maple or beech cane-seated chairs, you have no occasion to envy your neighbor her stuffed mahogany ones, which are probably as frail as they are uncomfortable.

The cost and room of a bookcase may often be saved by means of recesses in the walls, fitted with shelves.

In bedsteads simplicity is desirable. The broad foot-board is not only useless—it is often in the way. We hope to see a great reform in this article of furniture, and we have reason to think that it is already begun.

In selecting a carpet for a small room, avoid large figures, the effect of which is to diminish the apparent size.

In the initial cut of this chapter, the artist, following his own fancy, has given us a glimpse of an interior considerably beyond the range and style of our cottages. It shows how bright and pleasant a place a room may be made, and how much more sensibly thousands might live, who, with ample means to build and furnish as they please, spend their days in apartments dimly lighted, and stiff, and cheerless.

CHAPTER XV.

HINTS ON CONSTRUCTION.

 HE man who undertakes to build without any previous experience in that line, is liable to find himself involved in expenses for which he had made no calculation. A neglect of needful precautions in the earlier stages of the work,—neglect which his want of familiarity with such arrangements may naturally induce,—will perhaps seriously diminish the value of the structure.

The minutiæ of construction,—the modes in which building materials are to be shaped, combined, and adapted to their purpose, are to be sought for elsewhere ; as in the specifications of the architect, and in the knowledge and skill of the mason and carpenter. What the owner needs is, that his attention be seasonably called to certain things, which cannot be neglected without injury to his house.

It is not enough that he who proposes to build should have fully planned the structure, and that all its particulars are distinctly fixed in his own mind. This plan must be made equally clear to the mechanics who are to execute it. It should be so plain as to leave no chance for misunderstanding or perversion. And this requires that all the parts which can be so represented should be shown by drawings made to a scale sufficiently large to admit of measurement by the workmen. Every thing of importance for them to know, which cannot be drawn, should be fully described in writing. Floor-plans, showing the position and dimensions of walls and partitions; elevations, giving the form of each side, with the windows, doors, and other details; framing plans, determining the size and place of each stick of timber to be used; sections of mouldings, cornices, stairs, and all those parts which are of irregular outline; the whole accompanied by careful specifications of the quality of all materials, and the manner of their use,—are not only necessary in order to estimate, before building, what it will cost, but form the surest safeguard against misunderstandings, and against the taking of wrongful advantage when work is done by contract.*

Under whatever system mechanics may be employed, they are entitled to a reasonable compensation for the work which they perform, and the materials they supply. Yet amid the strifes of competition, or in times of business depression, contracts for building are often made at prices which both parties know, and one of them sensibly feels, to be too low. Such a course is injurious to both. To the mechanic, it is not only a compulsory sacrifice of what he ought to have, but also a strong temptation to do wrong. And however the employer may fancy that he gains by the closeness of his bargain, he is quite

---

* For the convenience of those who may adopt any of our designs, we have prepared working drawings. See card, following the Preface.

likely to prove the greater sufferer of the two. Not to mention the claims of justice and mercy,—though these should first be heard,—such transactions often prove unprofitable to the owner, resulting very naturally in his being put off with poor work and defective material. To deal only with those mechanics who have an established reputation for fidelity, as well as skill, is the true way to obtain the full value of your expenditure. With such a man, it matters little how your bargain is made. You may buy your own materials, and pay for the labor in day-wages, or at a stipulated sum ; or you may contract for materials and work at a given price. In either case, your own interest will be promoted by a close adherence to your original plan. Alterations, as we have said before, are very costly, and very vexatious. All this shows the need not only of a well matured plan, but also of a perfect understanding in the outset between the owner and the contractor. Let the bargain be well considered, and it will probably be faithfully carried out. Needless interference should be sedulously avoided. If the owner becomes convinced that the mechanic is not doing him justice, let them agree on some judicious neighbor to inspect the materials and work, and whose approval or rejection shall be final. In any event, keep clear of disputes, and especially of lawsuits.

The use of unseasoned lumber in building is a prolific cause of annoyance and damage. This is a matter which should be attended to in season. Better to pay six, or even twelve months' interest, insurance, and storage, than to build a hasty house of green stuff, and regret your folly every day you live. If the plan be determined on, the requisite quantity, sizes, etc., will be known. Whether you decide to build by contract, or otherwise, such provision may, and should be made. The seasoned stuff will always be good as cash in payment to the builder.

In reference to this point, some master builders always hold themselves in readiness for the proper erection of an edifice at short notice. To such we would suggest the propriety of securing, as they have opportunity, trunks of various trees which may be cut in their vicinity, or come within their reach. Somewhere, or somehow, they will all come in use.

We need not urge the proverbial importance of firm foundations. These should rest on an even surface of earth, below the reach of frost. The bottom, or foot course, should in general be flat, and broader than the wall placed on it. One benefit from this is the security which it gives against the undermining operations of rats ; the habit of this animal being to dig next the wall. For the same reason, this course should be a little below the bottom of the cellar. When practicable, foundation-walls should be made of square stones, the portion above ground being laid in mortar. Cellar walls should always be laid in mortar or cement.

A cellar should be dry and cool, but not so cold as to admit of freezing. Its dryness depends mainly on the situation and the nature of the ground. When these are such that water cannot otherwise be excluded, both the sides and bottom ought to be laid in cement. To prevent the air within from falling below the freezing point, that part of the wall which is above the surface, and also that which is in contact with ground that may freeze, should be made double, either by means of a distinct thin wall outside, or, more easily, by furring, lathing, and plastering inside ; the object in either case being to inclose between the partitions a thin space of air. This will not only retain the warmth in cold weather, but, in summer, will keep it out.

The frame of the house should be firmly bedded on the foundation walls. By a skilful use of mortar, where the walls meet the principal floor, all passage for rats and mice may be cut off. To secure dryness, there ought to be a considerable space under every lower floor for the circulation of air. It is not essential (though where it can be done it is best) to have a cellar under the whole house. But to bed any part of the building in the ground, as too many do, will conduce neither to its own health, nor that of its inhabitants.

WARMING AND VENTILATION are very important matters, demanding early and careful consideration. In regard to the former, the difficulty, in general, is not so much how to get the heat, as how to keep it. There can be no harm from the aggressive attacks of frost, so long as we keep its great antagonist at our side. To accomplish this, the external walls should be so constructed as to make them poor conductors of heat. In this respect, two thin walls, separated by a narrow stratum of confined air, are better than a very thick wall. The superior efficacy of air, when thus inclosed, as a non-conductor of heat, is perfectly established. In wooden buildings, the object may be accomplished by lathing and plastering *between*, as well as *on*, the studding, or by filling in with soft brick and mortar between the studding, leaving a thin space on each side.

It is on the same principle that windows are doubled. Not only does radiant heat pass easily through thin glass, but the glass itself, growing cold with the external air, rapidly abstracts heat from the inner air in contact with it. But put another thin glass before, or behind it, so that the air between, no matter how narrow the space, shall be tightly inclosed, and the remedy is perfect. This, therefore, should be regarded not as a luxury, but as necessary to comfort and true economy.

Wherever the winters are severe, the common, or living room, ought to be thus protected. Not only is fuel saved, and the whole room made more comfortable by such a provision, but the window itself, from being a dangerous, becomes a safe place to sit at. Especially is this important for delicate young women, who love to sit near the light as they read and sew, and thousands of whom have caught fatal colds in this very way.

An air-stratum of a quarter of an inch thickness is as effectual as one of three inches, and the object aimed at has been perfectly secured by doubling the glass in the same sash. The only objection to this is, that the inner surfaces will, after a while, need cleaning, but cannot be reached. This might be obviated by making the sash in two thin parts, to be held together by screws. To take them apart once or twice a year, and clean the interiors, would be a small affair. Such windows, if protected against the direct rays of the sun, and kept closed, would be as useful in summer by shutting out the heat, as they are in winter by keeping it within. The ungainly appearance of a large outside sash would thus be avoided, while the means of ventilation, and of using the open window, would be the same as with the ordinary single sash.

On economy in the modes of warming a house, much might be said. We can but glance at the fertile topic. We have great fondness for an open, and particularly for a blazing fire. So high is our estimate of its cheerful and healthy virtues, that we would forego many things, deemed important by some, rather than give up this dear old friend. As to close stoves, we like them so little, that we could preach against them with a will, and call them all manner of hard names. But, in this age of iron, what would it avail? The stove has become universal. All through the country, even where fuel is still abundant and cheap, it has supplanted the fireplace. Houses belonging to the class of our designs are generally so warmed. The cooking-stove, which, on the whole, is the least objectionable kind, from its supplying moisture as well as heat, is the only means of warming used in perhaps a majority of country and village houses. This being the case, plain stove-flues may, and doubtless will, be substituted for the fireplaces in some of these designs. For mere warming, we would recommend the open stove, standing out from the fireplace, as combining economy with comfort.

It will be noticed that we invariably place the chimney, not as it is usually, in the external wall, but in the central part of the house. This keeps in, and diffuses through the building, much heat, which, in the other case, goes immediately out of doors.

From the fact that heated air ascends, while that which is colder takes its place below, it is easier to warm the story above the fire than that in which it is placed. In this way, by very simple arrangements, the chambers, even in small dwelling-houses, may be cheaply warmed.

In cities, where the buildings are high, and close together, special means are needed to secure an ample supply and free circulation of air. In country houses, there is less occasion for such appliances, each room being in direct communication with a pure atmosphere.

Of the ventilators in general use, one class depends on creating a current of air in the building by the action of wind upon an external apparatus. It is some objection to these, that they fail at the very time when their service is most needed. Those modes of ventilation which depend on the ascending tendencies of heated air, are not only more uniform in their action, but more easy of application. In rooms, for instance, where stoves are used, good ventilation may be secured in the following simple and inexpensive way.

From a point, near where the stove is to stand, lay a pipe, or box, about six inches square, which shall communicate with the outer air. With this, connect another pipe, placed in a side or partition wall, and opening into the air-chamber of the roof. There should be an aperture in the latter pipe near the ceiling of the room. The stove must be so connected with the horizontal pipe that all other supply of air may be cut off at pleasure ; and both pipes must be properly furnished with valves. Suppose this arrangement to have been made in the kitchen. It is summer time ; the air of the room is not only warm, but surcharged with vapors and odors. Close the opening from the floor pipe to the outer air,—connect it with the upright one, and shut off this above the opening near the ceiling. The fire must now draw its sustenance from the air of the room, and taking it directly from the upper strata, which are most impure, will soon restore matters to a proper condition. But if there be no fire, by means of the floor pipe, introduce the outer air into the room, and leave open the passage to the roof. In rooms where there is nothing to make the air impure, supply the stove with fresh air from without, and cut off the communication with the side pipe. In parlors, or sitting rooms, during cold weather, the external air may in this way be made to pass round the fire, and thus enter the room pure, as well as warm.

But it is in bedrooms unprovided with fires, or flues, that the need of ventilation is most frequently perceived. Such rooms should be high, with an outlet at top for the escape of vitiated air. To protect upper rooms from the heating effect of the summer sun, and to secure the means of ventilation, a space of air should always intervene between the ceiling and the roof. This provision is made in all our designs. Reference to the accompanying section will show how this is done. A narrow air-space between the roof and plastered slope, is connected with the air-chamber at the peak. The air here, becoming heated, rises to the top, and escapes through apertures in each gable, just below the ridge. The current, which will usually set one way or the other, from opening to opening, will carry off the lighter and warmer air, which other-

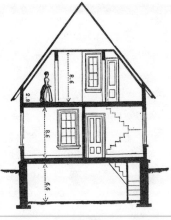

SECTION.

wise would render the rooms below all but intolerable. We have already alluded to the facilities which high-pitched roofs afford for securing coolness and ventilation, and now, again, invite attention to this, as well as to their other excellencies.

It is desirable that all windows, and very important that those of bedrooms should open at top, as well as at bottom. The extra cost of weights and pulleys (about two dollars a window) will never be regretted by those who shall experience the benefit.

A few of our plans, calculated for the vicinity of cities, and for villages where good mechanics are to be found, are made for tin roofs. The others are adapted to a shingle covering, as better, on the whole, for country houses.

Whenever (as in Design No. 2) the two sides of a roof meet at right angles, the shingles at the sloping ridge, or hip, should be laid with the courses of the two sides alternately overlapping each other. The peak of the roof should always be covered with ridge boards. The valley between two meeting roofs (as in Design No. 3) is to be covered with metal before shingling. For this purpose lead is preferable, but the "Terne" tin-plate answers very well. It should extend about ten inches under the shingles on each side, a space of some three inches wide being left unshingled in the centre. These directions are very important, as furnishing the best, if not the only security, against leaks. For the same reason, and in similar fashion, lead should be inserted in the courses of the chimney, where it meets the roof. If the latter be tinned, turn up the tin around the chimney, and build the edge of the sheet into the brickwork, about four inches above the roof.

In laying the chimney, and in framing the rafters, it must be borne in mind that the projecting base of the chimney-top, just below as well as above the roof, is larger than any other part of the shaft.

Health, comfort and decency, all demand that every dwelling, however humble, should have a water-closet under its roof, accessible with ease and without exposure to the external air. If the place be supplied with running water and facilities for drainage, such arrangements are made with very little trouble. The absence of these advantages involves the necessity of greater care, and perhaps cost, in the construction of vaults, etc. If the right

precautions are taken, all causes of offence will be effectually pre-
cluded. The partial and imperfect method by which many have
brought the water-closet under cover—methods which, through
ignorance or disregard of pneumatic laws, have converted the
whole house into a great flue for bad air—have undoubtedly pre-
judiced multitudes against all attempts of the kind. If there be
no sewer with which a connection can be made, a vault becomes
essential, and from this a chimney-pipe must open to the outer
air at a point above the ceiling of the apartment. In this way
an inverted syphon is formed, through the longer arm of which
the air-current will always set. This, be it remembered, is equally
important, whether the vault be under the common roof, or under
one that is detached and isolated, after the fashion which is so
common, so elegant, and so delicately conspicuous.

The use of timber in framing and building has been greatly
modified within the last few years. Economy and strength have
resulted from the change. It is now a principle well established,
that the power of timber to resist a cross strain is in proportion
to its depth rather than breadth. Acting on this, house-framers
now use stuff much smaller than the stout beams and posts which
our fathers supposed to be essential to strength and duration.
While this reduces the amount of timber used and the labor of
construction, it actually produces firmer and better work.

But this reform is not yet universal. In some parts of the
country, frames may still be seen with floor beams of perhaps
eight inches by six, laid with the broader side up, and two feet
apart. Instead of these, take plank eight inches wide and two
inches thick, and place them on edge, sixteen inches asunder.
This will save one half of the timber, while the floor laid thus will
sustain a third more weight. Indeed, if laid as first named, the

weight of the floor itself will cause it to settle. When the improved method is used, there should be diagonal cross braces
nailed between the beams, not only to keep them erect in their
places, but to distribute the resistance and prevent the floor from
springing. We may add in this connection that it is an excellent practice to *deafen* the floor ; that is, to fill a part of the
space between the floor beams with clay, or some other inelastic
and incombustible substance. This promotes warmth, renders
the floor less pervious to sound, and, in case of fire, will retard, if
it cannot stop the progress of combustion. The expense would
not be great, as the material is usually at hand, and no special
skill is required.

In the size of timber for the outside frame, a great reduc-
tion may be made on what many deem necessary, by placing
less dependence on its own stiffness and power to resist a cross
strain, and more on that of diagonal braces, and straight props
and ties, which resist in the direction of their length.

Because it is all to be covered up or for some other reason,
the preparation made for plastering is often very poorly done.
The studs, rafters, or furring, should not be too far apart ; the
laths should be good, properly spaced and firmly nailed. If the
laths are liable to spring or move, the " clinch " of the plaster
will break and there will be nothing to hold it on. Strips of
board, called " grounds," should be fixed at the sides of doors
and windows and at the floors as guides, enabling the plasterer
to make the surface plain and even. The carpenter is thus enabled to put on his trimmings without cutting away the mason's
work, or leaving crevices behind his own. It will be understood
that the trimmings are to be put on *after* the plastering, and
not before, as is the custom in some houses of a shabby and inferior character.

Shingled roofs are sometimes painted. It is a mistake to suppose that this makes them last longer. The paint, by creating small ridges or dams at the end of the shingles, where they join, tends to retain the water there and thus actually expedites decay. If the color be dark, as most generally it is, its absorbent properties cause the roof to become much hotter under a powerful sun. And finally, the paint does not improve its looks. This, it will be said, is a matter of taste. True, but we must have faith in our own. To our eye the unpainted roof, like the human head, grows handsomer with age, and we love to look at it, bleached by long exposure to sun and storm, and grown gray, as it were, in honorable service. Nor, if it still keep out the rain, would we wish to change it even when nature, with ever busy hand, has converted it into one of her own parterres, and covered its venerable surface with mosses and lichens.

With the outside walls of a wooden house the case is different. They should be well painted. Here as elsewhere true economy lies in using the best materials, and in employing only skilful workmen. Outside painting, to be lasting and handsome, should not be done in hot weather. The oil is then too readily absorbed. When it is cold, the oil and pigment slowly unite to form a tough and permanent coating. The necessity of repainting may long be deferred, by brushing over the surface with oil, every three or four years.

In regard to colors, there is a boundless diversity of taste, and this perhaps is well, for it insures variety. No rule can be given. Houses differing essentially in character and situation, ought not to be painted alike. White seems to be the general favorite. Yet this, for a near and constant object of sight, is not pleasing or kindly to the eye. Neither do we like, especially for rural dwellings, the darker shades. The needed variety may be found among the softer, lighter, and more cheerful tints ; tints which neither pain the eye by their glare, nor repel it by their gloom.

The scene around buildings in the process of erection is often very disorderly. This may be prevented by a little timely precaution. Let the owner designate, beforehand, places where the various materials shall be deposited, and mark out such space as may be needed for doing the work. The remaining part of the grounds and the trees, if it contain them, may be protected from injury, by a temporary fence. In his agreement with the builder, he should have a provision making him responsible for any damage that may accrue to his own or his neighbor's property through the carelessness or rudeness of the workmen.

Persons unaccustomed to watch the progress of a building, are liable to be deceived by its appearance in the earlier stages. The rooms look small and seem to be growing smaller, and very few things appear as they supposed they would. Hence often, needless apprehensions and worse than needless complaints. To such, we can only say that they are not competent judges in the case. All that they can do is patiently to await the completion of the structure. By that time, in all probability, their trouble and fears will have vanished.

CHAPTER XVI.

THE IMPROVEMENT OF GROUNDS.

 OWEVER great the success of the designer, and the care which is bestowed on the house, it will fall short of its proper and complete effect, if it be manifest that no attention has been paid to the grounds on which it stands. To this matter, accordingly, we devote a a few remarks.

The same obligation to regard truth and consistency,—the same duty of conforming to the circumstances of place and people, which we have urged in the formation of the house design, should also direct the arrangement and improvement of the grounds. But the diversities of soil and surface, of climate and exposure, are so numerous and great, that no one plan of improvement can be applicable to very many cases. Still, there are some principles and facts which are common to all ; and to these we ask attention.

GRADING.—All changes that are to be made in the -surface of the house-plot should be determined before the foundation is laid, though the work cannot be completely finished until after the house is done, and all rubbish is removed.

The position of the dwellings should be so adapted to the form of the ground as to permit, at all seasons, easy access from the street, and ready communication between different parts of the lots. The earth should slightly descend every way from the house, to lead off the water, and for its better appearance. But beware of making the slope too great. In this particular many err.

Various considerations, and, paramount among them, a regard for health, demand that early and judicious attention be given to the matter of drainage. All foul and waste water of the house should be carefully conveyed away. No water should be allowed to flow towards wells, yards, or buildings, nor to stagnate in pools, nor to run through walks, or garden paths.

What form the surface should be allowed to keep, or made to receive, depends much on the way it is to be used. For gardens, a southern exposure is generally preferable. If this be the object, and if the lay of the land is naturally unfavorable, much may often be done to improve it for the specific purpose, by throwing it into terraces, and by walls, which may serve both as support and protection. As a matter of ornament, however, we think that terraces should be sparely used. In general, a gentle inclination, or curved slope of ground, is far better on every account. It is difficult to preserve the greenness of a terraced bank in dry seasons ; it is more liable to be injured by heavy rains, and other violence ; it costs more to make at first, and more to keep it in order ; looks badly when it is not neat, and in its best estate is stiff and formal.

In the improving of rural grounds, it is desirable that the features which you introduce should harmonize with those which nature has already given. If the plot be quite small, and especially if the ground be level, this is a very simple affair. It becomes an important consideration, when the inclosure is sufficiently large to contain any considerable elevations and depressions, or prominent rocks, or large trees, or running or standing water. How are such things to be disposed of? With some persons, variety of this sort seems to be only another name for deformity. Their rule is, that the valley must be filled, and the hill brought low; that every thing which is crooked shall be made straight, and that all rough ways shall be made smooth. With reformers of this sort, who mar if they do not obliterate every thing that is expressive or picturesque in the grounds they occupy, we have no sympathy.

But he errs on the other side who leaves every thing in its native rudeness, and who, perhaps, even in his improvements, attempts to imitate the wildness of uncultivated nature. This last is, indeed, a vain endeavor.

In the immediate vicinity of our homes and in those objects on which the eye is constantly to rest, we need scenery which is tranquil and pleasing, rather than that which is wild and exciting. But let us have variety, if possible, and when Nature has kindly given it, let us not wilfully reject her aid.

Whether irregularities of surface shall be retained, or softened, or wholly removed, is a point which should be decided with reference to convenience.

We would not spare even an aged tree, if its retention would be prejudicial to comfort and especially to health. But when, with no such reason, for the sake perhaps of the fuel, or from mere recklessness and tastelessness, a man destroys, on his own ground, the magnificent plants which it has taken a lifetime or a century to rear, we can only say that he is a semi-barbarian.

Should your ground happen to contain a large boulder, or should some bed of rock crop out from its surface, do not, like many, suppose that a regard for good looks imposes on you the task of either blasting or burying the rugged intruder. Try rather, if it be not positively in the way of something needed and useful, to make it a pleasant feature in the scene. You may partially conceal it by vines or shrubbery. Half seen through leaves and clusters it will brighten, by contrast, the surrounding culture, and will remind each passer-by of toil performed and difficulties overcome.

Finally, does a brook meander through your small domain? If possible, suffer it still to wind and sparkle among the flowers and grass. We must plead for the innocent Naiad, free-born daughter of the hills. Force her not, henceforth, to creep darkly along between two straight, high, stone walls.

DISPOSITION OF GROUND.—To what special use each part of the ground shall be devoted, must depend in the main, on the size and situation of the lot, the nature of its soil and the form of its surface. Individual taste and local circumstances alone can decide how these useful and pleasing accessories shall be apportioned and arranged.

To say that the grounds and surroundings of a house should correspond with it in general character and expression, is but to repeat, in substance, what we have already urged. What we always wish to see, is an evident regard for simplicity, order, and neatness. Many attempt too much, crowding sometimes into a small plot what would be sufficient, if properly distributed and expanded, for five times the space.

While, in such matters, the convenience and pleasure of the occupants should first be thought of, their aspects, as seen by others, should not be disregarded. If practicable let the vegetable garden—which however useful is not beautiful—be screened from observation. Fruit trees will be safer at a little distance from the street, and they will also show better there.

Let it not be thought that we would discourage the cultivation of flowers, or that we are insensible to their charms, when we advise that the place devoted to them, should not be in front of the house. A flower-bed judiciously planted and well kept is, indeed a delightful spectacle, during the short season of its glory. But how short that is ! During times of drought, or conditions of neglect, sometimes unavoidable—during the witherings and decay of Autumn, and the long torpor of Winter—the case is very different, and the once smiling parterre becomes often actually repulsive. For these reasons, we would place the flower-garden where we can easily see it, if we choose, but shall not be compelled to see it always. The objection does not hold with reference to small patches of ever-blooming flowers, which cover the entire surface, (such as verbenas and portulaccas,) and which may be scattered here and there in the grass, or may serve to keep the ground open around small trees.

For an object of constant sight in front of the house and beneath its most occupied windows, there is nothing like grass. On nothing, probably, either in nature or art, can the eye rest with a delight so untiring and such ever new refreshment, as a smooth, thick carpet of green lawn, close-shaven and neatly kept.

The lawns of England have long been its pride and boast, —the wonder and admiration of all who visit that country. Many suppose that our drier and warmer climate makes it impossible for us to have these priceless ornaments of the landscape. There is a difficulty, unquestionably, but it is not insurmountable. Go anywhere in a time of drought, and mark the difference between a piece of American meadow land which has been deeply ploughed and highly manured, and the neighboring grounds, that have been tilled in the usual shallow and niggardly way. What a comfort to turn from these, all arid and brown, to the deep cool verdure of the other ! Take this lesson, and act upon it. Instead of covering a hard, sterile bed of earth, with lean sods of sour grass and sorrel from the wayside, spade deeply the plot which you intend for grass—pulverize it thoroughly—enrich it properly—plant, liberally, the right sort of seed—mow it every two or three weeks—give it, now and then, a rolling—keep it always clean—and we will insure you a carpet before your house that will infinitely outvie any you can spread within.

All this, indeed, involves some labor and some care. But it need not be expensive. Do the work yourself. Take care of it yourself. It will soon become a delight. And when you see your children playing on it, and the passing stranger stopping to take a pleased look at the beautiful sight, you will feel justly proud of your little green.

In the regards of every one who loves nature truly, trees must always fill a large place. It is not strange that our ancestors, who came here into the forest, and found its trees in their way, should have been anxious rather how to get rid of them, than how to preserve or plant them. Until within some twenty or thirty years very little was done in the way of setting out trees for shade or ornament, especially around houses. The change which has taken place, is very marked, and in many cases, very undesirable. In multitudes of our villages and smaller towns, not only are the streets lined with trees, but the yards of the dwelling houses are frequently filled with them. Their dense foliage brushes the windows, overhangs the roof, and wraps the habitation in perpetual shade. The opposite extreme of our ancestors was vastly better than this. The objections are—first and mainly—that it shuts out the light of day and the wholesome warmth of the sun, at times when they are much wanted. We have many cool and many stormy days during the period of leaves. At such times a house so surrounded is gloomy to live in and gloomy to look at. The shade and the humidity, which so many trees constantly maintain in and around the dwelling, is unfavorable to health. There can be no doubt of this. They obstruct, when dense, the free circulation of the air. Sometimes they fill the house with insects. Wooden roofs, when overhung by branches, rapidly decay.

Secondly—it does not look well. It is not in good taste, however it may be the fashion, thus to hide your house and hide your grounds behind a wall of leafage. In those lands where landscape gardening has been long cultivated, and where all points of this kind are carefully studied and well understood, this practice is very rare. The house is placed in sight, thrown open to the sun and air. Trees are set at a proper distance, where, from the house, they can be seen and admired. Is not this right? If not ashamed of your house, pray let it be seen.

"But how are we to shut out the sun in hot weather?" By projecting roofs, canopies, and verandahs; by door-blinds, and window-blinds, and curtains. There is no difficulty. Protect yourself against the sun by some shelter, which can be removed when again you want the sun. This is what you cannot do with your trees.

If the house stand near the street, and the street itself be lined with trees, these will generally furnish all that is needed in the way of shade. If the front yard be deep, and it is thought best to place a tree or two within it, we would recommend such as have a light, thin foliage, and do not attain to great size. The acacia and the mountain ash are examples of the kind.

We may add, in conclusion, that if you have many trees, and much shrubbery, you cannot have the lawn. Grass does not thrive under a dense shade, nor can it be properly cut and tended, where trees and shrubs interpose their obstructions. Within the actual circuit of the small grass-plot, it is very desirable that there should not be a single stem to interfere with the roller and scythe.

Finally, good friend, if you would have your house look inviting always to yourself, your family, and every body else, keep the grounds about it in perfect order.

In all these arrangements of a home, let not the children be forgotten. Give them a share in the garden, and teach them to raise roots and flowers. Let them have a right in the poultry-yard, and learn to feed their own fowls. Set apart some small place for a workshop, and accustom them early to the use of tools. Thus may they become timely industrious, trained to habits of skill, forecast, care, and thrift. Nor must the neces-

THE IMPROVEMENT OF GROUNDS.

sities of recreation be forgotten. It is as important that they should have time and place for play, as for work. If possible, let there be some appropriated spot, both within and without the house, where they shall feel at perfect liberty to enjoy themselves.

PATHS.—We have no desire to invade the province of the Landscape Gardener. But as most of those for whom we now write will feel unable to command his valuable skill, we offer a hint or two on the subject of paths. This is a branch of his labors, in which the professional artist sometimes finds it difficult to combine grace with utility. If, however, it is certain that one or the other must be sacrificed, we regard the case as clear. From the street to the house-door—from the kitchen to the well, or the stable—the communication should be direct as possible. Over paths that must be traversed many times a day, and often, perhaps, in hot haste, no one wishes to be compelled to describe lines of beauty, though Hogarth himself had drawn the graceful curve.

In gardens and pleasure walks the case is different, and we enjoy as a lawful luxury their easy windings and purposed prolongation. Yet even these should not be wholly capricious. Let there at least seem to be some reason for every turn—some compensatory attraction for every delay.

FENCES.—Though the fence ranks among the minor matters of building, it is far from being unimportant. Without it, no residence can be properly protected, or regarded as complete. Its style and condition often indicate, unmistakably, the taste and habits of the owner. What absurd fashions,—what strange and foolish fancies,—can be exhibited in fences, every observant traveller must often have remarked. And what surer sign of the sluggard, or the sloven, than leaning posts, gates that will not swing, missing rails, and broken palings ! And it is not the worst of it, that the eye is offended by absurdities and negligences in this particular. The imperfect barrier, and the neglected gateway, are a copious fountain of daily vexations, of serious injuries, and sometimes of quarrels and lawsuits.

That the fence should enhance rather than impair the effect produced by the house, it must be made to conform to it. This will best be done, not by a finical imitation of details, but by imparting to it the same general character, whether of simplicity or richness, of lightness, or of strength. A fence should be adapted not only to the house, but to the location and the neighborhood. Before you copy some pattern, which has struck your fancy, consider whether the circumstances of the two are alike. A rich fence of wood, or iron, in some rude forest situation, and a mock rustic one, of unbarked cedar, on a city street, are about equally appropriate.

To shut from view a stable-yard,—to protect a garden, or fruit orchard, from noxious winds, or marauding bipeds, a high, close fence, is often reared. But avoid such a fence, unless the demand is imperative. High, close fences, around houses and pleasure grounds, have a niggardly, exclusive, prison-like aspect. A fence may secure the place from intrusion, and yet afford free passage to air and light. If practicable, let your fences be of the open sort, and then, so far as sight is concerned, others will enjoy your grounds as much as yourself. This is an easy benevolence, but, alas ! how few practise it ! High, close fences are often used for the separation of contiguous lots. But why ? They are promotive neither of good looks, nor good feelings. Some slight railing, or invisible fence of wire, is in better taste, both æsthetically and morally.

All necessary divisions of the plot itself, whether temporary or permanent, should obstruct the view as little as possible. For such purposes the wire fence answers well. It is quickly placed, quickly removed, and cheap withal.

Woven wire fence stuff is now made at very moderate cost, and will last a good while, if kept well painted. This will do very well for the front fence of a small door-yard.

There is, probably, no inclosure, in all respects so pleasing, as a quick-set hedge, properly shaped and neatly kept. Any body may have one who is willing to give time and attention to such matters. No need of sending to distant nurseries, or seed stores, for some exotic plant. Almost any of our native trees may be grown in hedges. The apple, for instance, will make an excellent fence, durable and impervious. But evergreens are preferable. The arbor-vitæ, the hemlock, the spruce, and the fir, may easily be obtained, and their green walls will give pleasure all the year round. But let no careless, slovenly man ever attempt to have a live hedge. All its beauty and virtue depend on its being well preserved and constantly cared for. When neglected, straggling, and broken, it becomes a most unsightly and useless object.

We come now to wood fences, which are far more frequent than any other. The facility and quickness with which they are put up—their cheapness and showiness—are their strong recommendations.

In making such a fence, it is of the first importance that the posts be firmly set. To this end, let the hole be of the smallest possible diameter, and twice as deep as frost ever reaches. Throw in slowly round the post, earth free from stones, ramming it solidly all the time.   There is some trouble in this, but it pays in the end.   If the post be set with its natural top downward, the reversal of the sap vessels will retard the absorption of water, and will thus add to the durability of the timber.

A disordered rickety gate is an occurrence so common and so annoying, that we expect to be thanked for a word or two on this point.   The trouble may result from various causes, such as instability of the posts, want of strength and proper bracing in the gate-frame, insecure attachment of the hinges, and a poor or dislocated catch.   Sometimes the distance between the gate-posts is not rightly adjusted, or the ground below has not been properly graded.   Let all these things be carefully looked to, in time.   Be sure that your gate has the best of stuff, and the best of work. If much used, it should be provided with some simple, self-acting fastener.

Unless you wish to invoke curses on your head, both loud and deep, don't let your gates swing outward !

From the boundless variety of wooden fences, we select two or three, which we can commend as neat, simple, and economical.

It is an improvement on the common form of the picket fence, to use pickets more than an inch thick, and but little wider than that, so that the tops shall be nearly square.   The accompanying cut presents a still better modification, suitable for the separation of lots.   The palings are thick, six feet in length, inclosed between double rails, so that the fence has the same aspect on both sides. Train along such a fence the Wistaria vine, and in the season of bloom, you will have a lovely wall of verdure, surmounted by a glorious cornice.

For their inclosures many use the common "fencing-lath" of the lumber yards. But these are neither straight nor thick enough to make a good fence in the ordinary way. They may, however, be turned to account in the following manner.

Place the lath with their sides toward each other; cut grooves in the under side of the upper rail, to receive their ends, and cover the joints on both sides with narrow moulding strips. Secure them at the foot by three narrow strips, as shown in the section.* To make the central blocks which separate the laths, take an inch board, three inches wide; with an inch and a half auger, bore holes four inches apart, and saw through the holes.

SECTION.

In the neighborhood of cities, and wherever a needy and unscrupulous population is found, fences secured by nails only, stand but a poor chance. As offering more protection against these petty thieves, we suggest the accompanying and the following patterns. Their decided advantage in point

---

* The cuts of fences are all made on a scale of one quarter of an inch to a foot, except the section, which is three times the size.

of appearance will be at once apparent. Fence like this, with moulded rails and round balusters, all accurately made by machinery, is now manufactured at Buffalo, and sold, not only

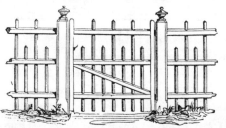

there, but in New York and elsewhere, for less than the-cost of common picket fence.

We give here another form, with three rails and heavier balusters—as one of the many variations, which may be made in this sort of fence.

It is obvious that the color of the fence should conspire with its form and other qualities, in making it only a subordinate feature of the place.

DRAINAGE.—A general allusion to this important topic is hardly sufficient. Should any part of your ground be springy ; especially should you find that water is likely to ooze from that which is under and near the house, resort must be had to underdraining. In the same way treat every low and swampy spot, where water stands. This, remember, is a question of health, as well as of comfort, and admits no alternative. In the case of swampy ground it becomes also one of gain.

There are many ways of draining ; such as by trenches partially filled with small stones ; by sewers of brick ; by clay pipe and clay tile. You must determine for yourself what mode is best in your own case.

If there be no provision for retaining and using the rainwater, an under drain of stones or some other precaution is needed, to prevent the descending streams of the roof from washing away and disfiguring the surface.

For the waste water of the kitchen there should be a covered drain. This water is valuable, and should not be lost. If practicable, let it flow into a manure vat, at some distance from the house, into which earthy and vegetable materials should occasionally be thrown. These will absorb it, and thus become rich fertilizers. If this cannot be, it may discharge into some brook—or in default of this, into a covered cess-pool, sunk in porous earth. To prevent it from becoming a thoroughfare and retreat for rats, guard it at each end by coarse gauze of copper wire.

Still more important is a stench-trap at the entrance, to seize and hold its foul and noxious odors. Millions, for want of this simple contrivance, breathe mephitic vapors every day—and it is impossible to doubt that many, many thousands of human beings have sickened and died from thus needlessly, but constantly, inhaling the poisonous gases of sinks and sewers.

But what is a stench-trap ? some may possibly ask. A very slight affair. Here is one. *a* is a hopper-shaped wooden box to receive the waste water ; *b* is the drain or trough that takes it  away ; the partition *c* reaches far enough below the under edge of the trough to cut off all air communication between *a* and *b*. It is in fact an inverted syphon, whose bend being always full of water, allows no air to pass. These traps ready-made of terra-cotta, may be obtained at the manufactories and warehouses of that article.

Clay pipe, which may be procured in short pieces of any diameter required, is the best material for such drains. Once in the ground it is literally imperishable. But when these cannot easily be got, troughs of yellow pine, or of chestnut plank do perfectly well.

CISTERNS.—We had occasion in an earlier chapter, to touch on the excellencies of rain-water. Strange to say, they seem to be comparatively unknown. The vast alembic of the atmosphere is unceasingly at work, in distilling from the salt sea brine a pure crystal element. From its magazines of cloud, that element is again dispensed and distributed over the earth, and with absolute certainty, if not with entire regularity. There are very few places on this globe of ours, where the supply from the heavens— coming either at irregular intervals, or in one or two seasons of continuous rain, is not sufficient, if collected and preserved, for the entire domestic uses of the people.

Rain comes to us pure, or nearly so. We do not have to go after it ; it seeks us. On the palace and the cottage roof alike it lays its benignant offering—seeming to patter—" Here I am. Set your tanks, and they shall be filled." But how often is this offer scorned. Off it runs and sinks speedily into the more grateful earth. Down through vegetable mould, through masses of drift, and fissures of the partially soluble rock, it silently makes its way, taking up something from each as it goes. At length some clay bed arrests and accumulates the waters.

And now we, who saw this pure liquid go down before our faces, and had only to reach forth our cups and catch it,—what do we wise folks do ? We dig, we bore, we blast ; often at great expense and with much labor, we penetrate deep into the bowels of the earth, till we reach the water. Then we insert a pump, or rig a windlass, and work hard to lift a little of it up. And what do we get ? A lixivium—a solution of salts—sulphates and carbonates—chlorides and iodides—and ever so many more. Almost all well water is mineral water. Much of it is absolutely unfit to use ; gradually deranging the system, and acting as a slow poison.

The rain falling on roofs upon which soot and dust constantly gather, must carry with it to the reservoir these impurities. And hence, much of the prejudice which exists against the use of rainwater as a drink, and in cooking. Multitudes have never seen it clear and sweet, and do verily seem to think that it is foul when it comes down. How then is it to be made fit for use?

Various processes have been devised for the filtering of impure water. One is to insert the foot of the pump into a mass of porous stone, through which the water must percolate before it enters the pump. Another is to attach a filterer to the muzzle. Filtering vessels are also manufactured, differing much in kind, size, and merit. Into these the impure water is poured, and drawn off clear below. Some of these answer an excellent purpose, and should certainly be obtained by those who, from any cause, do not choose to secure the desired end in the cistern itself.

But a filtering cistern is, on the whole, far preferable to any other method. One way is to make a partition, a, in the cistern,

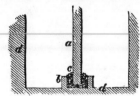

dividing it into two portions. This partition is pierced at the bottom with several apertures. A low wall, b, is built up on each side the partition, and a few inches above the top of the apertures. The open space between these low walls, c, is filled with charcoal broken fine, and with gravel—the latter being on top. The water is conducted into one apartment, and may always be drawn up bright and clear from the other. The accompanying section, to which the letters have reference, may help to make this account more intelligible.

We have lately seen what appears to us a decided improvement on the plan just described. In this the filtering cistern is a separate affair. A cask, holding perhaps a hundred gallons, is placed by the side of the larger cistern, and quite near the surface of the ground. An aperture in its bottom, over which is secured a large sponge, is connected by a good-sized pipe of wood or clay, with the main tank. A third part of the cask is now filled with the charcoal and gravel ; the conductor from the house is led into it, and the thing is complete.

This mode is not only as easy and as cheap as the other, but has this great advantage, that the filterer can be often and readily cleaned, while in the other case, it is necessary to remove all the water and to go down deep, in order to accomplish the work.

Brick cisterns covered with cement, are better and more durable than wooden ones. When the ground is of such a nature that a smooth cylindrical hole can be made in it without much trouble, there is no need of brick. First cover the bottom with a bed of concrete—then set up a curb of boards around, leaving a narrow space between it and the earth, and fill in with your liquid concrete. It will soon harden into stone, and if the work be well done, will stand till the earthquake comes. If you use the small wooden filterer, let that also be bedded in concrete.

We cannot apologize for having thus stepped perhaps a little out of our professional walk, nor for having dwelt with what may be deemed needless minuteness on a subject which to some will seem of trifling moment. It does not so appear to us. We cannot resist the conviction that the water which men drink, has almost as much to do with their health, as the air they breathe. A large portion of our vast country rests on strata of limestone. Wherever this is the case, the water is more or less impregnated with salts of lime. Multitudes have and seek no other drink, than the turbid waters of western streams. To these causes is undoubtedly to be attributed much of the sickness which prevails in those regions. The highest authority of science and experience assures us that the free use of such water predisposes the drinker to attacks of cholera, and makes that now constant terror of the West more malignant and fatal.

For all this, how obvious the remedy ! How prompt ! How easy ! and how cheap !

HOUSE PLOT.—It is rather to illustrate some of the ideas presented in this chapter, than as a pattern for exact imitation, that we give a plan of arrangement for a small village lot. It is supposed to be level ground on the east side of the street. It is seventy-five feet in front, by one hundred and fifty deep. Though larger than lots usually are in our new suburban villages, it is not large enough for satisfactory cultivation in a general way.

We suppose the house, Design 11, to be placed in the centre of the lot, twenty-five feet from its front. The verandah and the parlor front windows look toward the west. The hall and kitchen windows and the rear entrance face the south ; this being the position which is best adapted for comfort at all seasons of the year, and all hours of the day.

Along the northern side of the lot runs a straight lane for communication with the stable. This, which is wide enough for a load of hay to pass, is turfed and separated from the rest of the land by a wire barrier. A grape vine, protected by a bar or light railing, is trained along the fence.

There are two gates in front, opening into paths about three and a half feet wide, which bending with easy curvature, meet in front of the verandah. A continuation leads to the rear entrance, and thence by the well to the stable. Branches from this diverge, and reunite on the south side of the garden. Regularity is aimed at in the lines of the front yard, as in good keeping with the character of the house and its verandah. The semicircular space *c* is laid down to grass, with no obstructions upon it but the

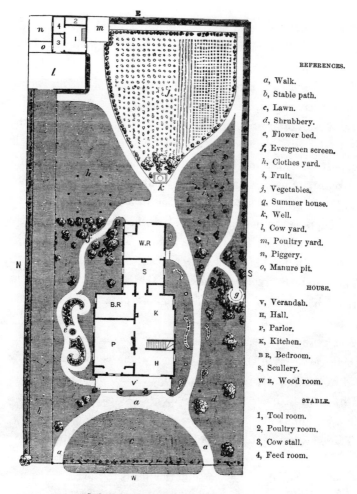

REFERENCES.

a, Walk.
b, Stable path.
c, Lawn.
d, Shrubbery.
e, Flower bed.
f, Evergreen screen.
h, Clothes yard.
i, Fruit.
j, Vegetables.
g, Summer house.
k, Well.
l, Cow yard.
m, Poultry yard.
n, Piggery.
o, Manure pit.

HOUSE.

V, Verandah.
H, Hall.
P, Parlor.
K, Kitchen.
B R, Bedroom.
S, Scullery.
W R, Wood room.

STABLE.

1, Tool room.
2, Poultry room.
3, Cow stall.
4, Feed room.

Scale 32 feet to an inch.

small flowering shrubs that skirt the fence. The portion on the right of this may have a few fruit trees, with here and there, if you like, a choice shrub. If preferred, a suitable shade tree may be planted at each corner of the lot, next the street.

The walks, it will be seen, allow one to traverse nearly the whole ground, without returning on his steps. On the northern side is a small flower bed of fanciful shape. Several little beds of various form are cut in the grass near the principal walk, for the cultivation of petunias, verbenas, portulaccas, violets, myrtles, and other plants of similar character. Each bed must be planted with but one sort, which must fill and cover the entire spot.

The ground next to the house is kept in grass, or devoted to creeping vines ; of which there is one at the foot of each verandah post. A shrub shades the bedroom window.

In a part somewhat secluded is placed the summer-house, or garden seat, *g*. The well-house, *k*, is also partially embowered. A small thicket of evergreens at *f* shuts off from the street a sight of the clothes-yard. Its hedge-like character is disguised in front by the irregularity of the planting.

The plot, *i*, may be devoted to berries, or fruits. Borders of currants, raspberries, etc., extend from the summer-house to the south-east corner, and also hedge in the vegetable garden. Trailing plants may be made to cover the stable-yard fence, which is supposed to be a close one.

In the vegetable garden it would be well to raise only the choice roots and plants of household use in summer. It were better to obtain potatoes, and other winter supplies of vegetables, from some cheaper ground. The clothes-yard may be used, if necessary, for the temporary deposit of wood, and the space in its rear is a play-place for the children.

The stable is designed to be a square building, with hipped roof and battened sides. The upper story should be high enough to contain a sufficient supply of hay, with a window in front for its reception. On the first floor is a large room for the storage of tools, and for general purposes. The hen-house (2) has an opening into the yard, *m*, and is provided with boxes for nests, which open from the tool-room. There is a stall for the cow, and her manger is so placed that it can be supplied from the tool-room. A door in the same room opens at the right hand of the cow. No. 4 is a feed-room, from which the hog receives his rations.

The yard, *l*, slopes towards the manure pit, *o*. This insures a dry bed for the cow. She should also have the shelter, in summer nights and stormy winter days, of a low shed, which may be built against the stable wall.

The well is conveniently placed for supplying house, stable, and garden.

THE STREET.—Interest and duty should alike prompt you to pay some attention to that part of the highway which adjoins your premises. Do not subject yourselves and others to perpetual vexations, because the authorities of the place neglect their duty. As far as your own line extends, make and maintain a wide, smooth, dry side-walk, with a gradually sloped water-course between it and the carriage-way. Let there be against your ground no unsightly, or dangerous banks. Let no needless obstructions, or rubbish, ever deform your side of the road. The outer edge of the side-walk is usually the proper place for trees. Select them judiciously. There is a wide range of choice. Plant them also judiciously. It is a mistake to set them thickly, with the idea of thinning out, when they become large. The process is hardly ever performed. Let the uncrowded tree spread itself in the air and light, and its top will become full, symmetrical, and beautiful. Beware of the pruning knife. Ornamental trees are often spoiled in this way.

At a proper distance from the gate, place a hitching post, provided with a chain halter. It will save your side-walk, your fence, and your young trees from harm ; and, perhaps, it will save your own, or your neighbor's horse and carriage.

In regard to such improvements as these, do not wait for others to lead the way. Set the example, and say nothing. Your neighbors must be different from most men, if they long resist such teaching.

CHAPTER XVII.

THE GARDEN.

GARDENING, though it has much increased in extent and favor, is still far from being an object of general attention among us. With the majority of our rural and village population, it is a thing almost wholly neglected. They have every facility. But the willing soil lies untilled at their very doors, while sunshine and shower, with all their fertilizing and fruit-producing powers, fall unavailingly on the neglected ground.

The taste is wanting. The culture of salads and pulse, of roots, fruits, and flowers, has not yet become the fashion. The material advantages, one would think, the saving and the profits, might induce many to have a good garden. The truth is, that they are content with a meagre board. They forego altogether the cheap dainties of the garden, rather than take the trouble to raise them.

To say nothing of these,—its innocent luxuries,—a well-kept garden is a feast for the eye. The fragrance of its flowers and fruits regales the sense of smell. Its culture is an easy and pleasing occupation for both youth and age. Portions of its care are well adapted to the quick eye and delicate hand of woman. The employment which it furnishes is healthy, as well as agreeable. As a pleasant resort, and an object of just pride, it tends greatly to strengthen the ties of domestic attachment. To sum up,—a neat, productive garden, tended by the family itself, is not only one of the most delightful things about a homestead, but one of the best. It is a moral power—pure, wholesome, and conservative.

Gardening is a pursuit which, once taken up, is apt to grow in the love of its votaries. There is good reason for this. The practical horticulturist is constantly making progress in knowledge and skill. The results of his industry and care are visible and tangible results. He finds his experience growing yearly more profitable, as well as pleasing. Of necessity, he becomes attached to objects which he has aided in calling into being, and has tended with so much care. No other tree can interest him like that which he himself planted, or grafted. Its health, its growth, its annual putting forth of buds and leaves, and flowers and fruits, are watched by him with a solicitude, not wholly unlike that which he feels for his children, who are growing up with it.

Do not suppose that experience and knowledge are necessary in order to make a beginning, nor think that unless you can have a large and complete garden, it is not worth your while to have any. Many err from attempting too much. The first results are unsatisfactory, and they give up the attempt in disgust. No more ground should be set apart for this purpose than can be thoroughly attended to. A large, neglected, slovenly garden, will yield neither pleasure nor profit. Begin, then, moderately ; but do not forget that your requirements will increase with your experience and skill. Your plans in this respect should have reference to the future, as well as the present.

Set out with a determination to cultivate only the best plants, fruits, etc. These occupy no more space, and require no more care, than those of an inferior quality. Especially is this incumbent on those whose garden room is small. There will be more of pleasure, and of profit too, in the thorough and successful culture of a few choice sorts, than in the production of a great variety.

The few hints which we venture to offer on the subject of gardening will be mainly of a preliminary and precautionary character. We would point out certain steps which should be taken at the outset. For the details of practice, there is no teacher like experience ; or if other aid be needed, there are treatises in abundance.

For the substance of these suggestions, for the flower-bed designs, and lists of plants and fruits, we are indebted to the kindness of a gentleman well known for his skill and taste in horticulture.*

The first matter of importance is the preparation of the soil. The aspect, grading, etc., must, of course, depend on the circumstances of each case. The ground, whether meant for garden or lawn, should be spaded from two to three feet down, and

---

* Peter B. Mead, Esq., Secretary of the New York Horticultural Society, and late Corresponding Secretary of the American Institute.

cleared of stones. It may be done in this way. At one end of the ground to be dug mark off a strip,—say three feet wide. From this remove the earth a spade's depth, throwing it on the outside. Stir the bottom of this trench another spade's depth, and pick out the stones. Now mark off a second strip, and spade as before, throwing the earth into the trench just made. Loosen the bottom of the second trench, and so proceed till the whole is dug. The earth removed from the first trench must be used to fill the last one. It will take longer, but will generally pay well, to throw out from each trench two spits deep, stirring the bottom as before.

The importance of this process is well understood by practical gardeners, and can hardly be overrated. It gives a chance for the roots to descend, and by allowing air and moisture to penetrate, furnishes not only nourishment, but warmth.

In this process of trenching, many small stones will be thrown out. These are of great value in making walks. Having marked out the path, excavate the whole of it to the depth of three feet. Fill up one foot with stones ; the largest below. Upon the stones place a layer of brush, or of sods ; then a foot of soil, to be topped with gravel, slightly crowned. The bed of stones and brush will not only keep the path dry and hard at all times, but will serve the valuable end of draining the adjoining ground. Where anthracite coal is burned, the ashes make a good covering for garden and other paths, treading down hard, and keeping out grass and weeds.

If the ground be naturally wet, it may need additional underdraining, which can be effected by other trenches of the same kind, or by the use of tile.

How little patches for flowers may be cut in the green turf, and how they should be planted, we have already shown. We also gave, in the Design for grounds, an ornamental flower bed. Two other specimens of geometric figures for the same purpose, by Mr. Mead, are here presented. They are intended to show what may be done. There is no limit to the variety of such combinations. The figures are easily formed. Two sharpened sticks, connected by a string, are the only instruments required. One of the figures, it may be seen, is numbered and lettered.

Scale 16 ft. to an inch.

A selection of plants, proper for each spot, and so arranged with reference to size, colors, etc., as to produce a pleasing and harmonious effect, will be found in the following instructions :—

In the middle of one of the outer borders plant Magnolia purpurea, and in the middle of the corresponding borders, Rhus cotinus, Euonymus Americanus, and Viburnum opulus,—all large shrubs. Midway between these and the corners, plant Halesia tetraptera, Rhododendron catawbiense, Philadelphus gracilis, Chionanthus virginicus, Clethra alnifolia, Kalmia latifolia, Hibiscus Syriacus, Weigela (Diervilla) rosea. Between these last and the first named, plant Azalea Pontica, Styrax glabra, Forsythia viridissima, Lonicera Tartarica, Aucuba Japonica, Euonymus Japonica, Mahonia aquifolia, and Coronilla emerus. In the central points of the same borders, plant an Azalea, Spiræa callosa, Mahonia aquifolia, and Euonymus Japonica variegata. In the four corners, plant Syringa Josackii, Philadelphus coronarius, Halesia diptera, and Deutzia scabra. There will still be room enough for other plants, but they must not be crowded; this room may be occupied with Calycanthus floridus, Berberis purpurea,

Yucca gloriosa, Spiræa thalictroides, S. trilobata, S. Douglassii, Cotoneaster microphylla, Dielytra spectabilis, Cratægus pyracantha, and some choice roses. The paths indicated by the dotted lines in the corners may be omitted or opened, as desired.

In the middle of the centre piece plant the Spiræa Reevesii, and in the centres of the beds 2, 3, 4, and 5, plant roses—Geant des Battailles, Caroline de Sansal, Prince Albert, and Pius IX. In each' of these beds, at equal distances apart, and about one foot from the edge, plant three of the following: Spiræa filipendula, Plumbago larpentæ, Anemone Japonica, Crucianella stylosa, Myosotis palustris, Hepatica trilobata, Dodecatheon meadia, Alyssum saxatile, Convallaria majalis, Aquilegia glandulosa, Sedum Sieboldii, and Chelone barbata.

The position of plants in each of the beds numbered 6, 7, 8, and 9, is to be according to the letters shown on that marked 8; and the sorts as follows:—At a, Roses—Hermosa, Mrs. Bosanquet, La Reine, and Augustine Michelet; at i and c, Phloxes; at d, an Antirrhinum; at h, a Delphinium; at f, Lychnis Chalcedonica, Dictamnus rubra, Pentstemon gentianoides, and Campanula grandiflora; at e, Valeriana rubra, Œnothera Frazerii, Lychnis viscaria, and Veronica spicata; at g, Pentstemon atropurpureum, Lupinus polyphyllus, Aconitus napellus, and Aconitum speciosum; at b, Dracocephalum speciosum, Valeriana officinalis, Spiræa lobata, and S. Americana.

In addition, there should be distributed about the borders a good collection of Chrysanthemums. In the fall, clumps of Tulips, Hyacinths, Narcissuses, Jonquils, and Crocuses, may be planted wherever room may be found for them. Bedding plants are indispensable. Among the best are Verbenas, Petunias, Cupheas, Scarlet Geraniums, Nierembergias, Gaillardias, etc. Also Dahlias, Gladioluses, etc.

A similar arrangement of the same plants, with such modifications as circumstances and good taste may dictate, will be readily made for the beds of the design on the next page.

We commend this delightful task to the young, and especially to young women. The examples furnished will soon suggest others, and they will find occupation ever fresh and pleasing, in devising new combinations of figure, and new arrangements of flowers.

The fruit and vegetable garden should be laid out in large squares, in order that no room be needlessly occupied by walks. Every inch of valuable ground should be devoted to some useful purpose. Let these squares be edged with box, kept always neatly trimmed. Dwarf fruit trees (especially the pear) may be planted on all sides of these squares—about four feet from

the box edging, and from six to eight feet apart. Between every two trees, a currant or gooseberry bush may be planted. A part of one square may be appropriated to an asparagus bed, a portion of another may be set apart for strawberries. Against the fences, raspberries and blackberries may be plant- ed. Across the middle of one square, a row of rhubarb plants may be set—not less than four feet apart.

Wherever the climate allows, every body should raise grapes. They occupy but little ground. They will grow in corners, and by the side of buildings, where nothing else of value could stand. They will run up your verandah posts, and stretch along the cornice, and adorn with their green drapery and purple clusters, the otherwise blank and unsightly wall. By no other culture, with the same ground and the same care, can we obtain so much of gratification both for the eye and the palate.

Grapes should be propagated from eyes and cuttings, and not from layers. They should have, if possible, a southern ex- posure. They may be grown either on a trellis or an arbor. The trellis is by far the best. For this you may set posts, six to eight feet out of ground. Then through holes in these, about two feet apart, run strong annealed wire, and wedge it fast. Plant the vines from eight to ten feet apart, and prune them annually and thoroughly on the cane system. This is an important operation, and he, who has had no experience, will do well to employ, for the first time, some practiced hand. Autumn, as soon as the leaves have fallen, is the best time for pruning grape-vines.

Fruit trees should be planted in the fall, after the leaves have fallen. If not covenient to plant at this time, the operation may be deferred till early spring. Great care should be taken of the roots and small fibres. The holes should be large enough to allow them to spread out in their natural position. Many err in planting too deep. Fruit trees do not flourish unless, like other plants, they are cultivated. The ground around them should be well worked, occasionally top-dressed, and kept free from grass and weeds.

The benefits which result from pruning fruit trees and shrubs, are not appreciated as they ought to be. Many seem to be afraid of the knife and saw. They cannot bear to cut away so much good wood, or to destroy so many buds that might ripen into fruit. But long and large experience have shown that in no other way can the best results be reached. To shape the tree—to lay it open for the admission of air and light—to hasten its bearing, and to improve its fruit in size and quality—are the objects and results of judicious pruning.

Fruit trees may be pruned at any time during winter, or early in spring, before the sap begins to run. Summer pruning should be confined to repressing shoots of too luxuriant growth, by pinching out the terminal eye, and thinning out branches where they are too thick. But this is sometimes carried too far.

Leaves have an important agency in the ripening process, and it is injurious to remove those which are near the fruit. The fruit of pear and other trees may often be thinned out, to the great improvement of that which is left.

Currants and gooseberries should be grown to single stems—tree-form. They may be propagated from cuttings of the last wood (not so well by suckers) before growth begins in spring, or early in September. Rub out all the eyes excepting three or four at the top. For general purposes we commend the large Dutch currant. Others will be found in our list. The wood of currants should be thinned out and cut back.

It has been difficult to raise the gooseberry in this country, from its liability to mildew. There is an American variety (Houghton's seedling) which, according to our experience, is not open to this objection. We treat it as follows. At the bottom of the hole we place a mixture—one part of wood mould and two parts of old rotten manure. In the fall we top dress, and take care, especially in dry weather, to keep the soil open and porous. Gooseberries should be pruned late in the fall, or early in spring.

As soon as the fruit of your raspberries is all gathered, cut down to the ground the stems which bore it, that the suckers, which are to be the fruit-bearers of the following year, may get air and light. These also, when numerous, should be thinned out. In spring, the lateral, or side branches, should be shortened in about a third of their length, and all dead wood removed. Some raspberries need to be covered during winter.

For ASPARAGUS, place about six inches of manure at the bottom of the bed, with a light vegetable mould above. The crown of the plant should not be more than three inches below the surface ; only that part which is above the ground is fit to eat. An occasional top-dressing of salt is beneficial. In fall, cover the beds with manure—not for protection, but for enrichment. The smallest family will need for this edible at least a square rod. There is no better mode of forming an asparagus bed than to plant the seed at once in the bed. When the plants are well up, thin them out, so as to stand a foot apart in the rows ; the latter should be about 18 inches apart.

STRAWBERRIES.—In a small garden it is not well to grow many kinds, and these should be selected in reference to size, flavor, and productiveness combined. Foreign varieties do not succeed well with us ; our intense summer heat burns them up. A good selection may be made from the following : *— Hovey's Seedling, (P.) ; Longworth's Prolific, (H.) ; McAvoy's Superior, (P.) ; Boston Pine, (H.) ; Monroe Scarlet, (P.) ; Scott's Seedling, (H.) ; Moyamensing, (P.) ; Walker's Seedling, (H.) ; and Burr's New Pine, (P.)

The best soil for strawberries is a heavy loam, to which has been added a good proportion of vegetable mould from the woods. A new soil,—an inverted sod, for example,—suits them best. The manure used should be old and well rotted, and thoroughly incorporated with the soil, which should be trenched two or three feet deep. An occasional top-dressing of ashes is beneficial. Beds are made in various ways. One of the best, for a small garden, is to place the plants a foot apart each way in a bed three feet wide, beginning at six inches from the edge,

* The letters H. and P. denote respectively Hermaphrodite and Pistillate. The Hermaphrodites will fruit by themselves—the Pistillates will not ; and this is why we sometimes see beds entirely unproductive, no regard having been paid to their sexual character. Let it be borne in mind that Pistillates will not produce a crop of berries unless Hermaphrodites are planted near them. They need not be in the same beds, but near by.

leaving a walk eighteen inches wide between the beds. A pistillate variety may be planted in one bed, and an hermaphrodite in another. Beds may be made at almost any time, provided the plants are watered when the weather is dry. It is better to plant immediately after a rain. September and early spring are the best seasons. Plants put out in September, and even in October, will yield a fair crop the following spring. If carefully done, a tolerable crop may be had from plants put out in early spring. In the fall, give a top-dressing of manure between the rows. A slight covering of hay or straw will prevent the plants from being lifted by repeated freezings. No runners must be allowed to grow. Stir up the ground as soon as the frost is out, and put a little clean hay or straw on the ground to keep the berries clean. A bed carefully made, and well kept, ought to be productive five or six years.

Whether in the vegetable, fruit, or flower garden, let it be remembered that the ground cannot be too frequently stirred, especially in dry weather.

There should be in the vegetable garden a central walk, about four feet wide, for the passage of a wheelbarrow. For the other walks, a width of two and a half to three feet will suffice.

A rose trellis, or an evergreen hedge, makes an appropriate screen between the flower and the vegetable gardens.

Over the summer-house, if there be one, train the monthly honeysuckle.

For piazza columns and cornice, and for the corner-posts of houses, the Wistaria sinensis, the Bignonia radicans, and the Bignonia grandiflora, are suitable and beautiful ornaments. So also are some of the running roses.

While you are building for yourself, build also for the birds. They are the natural friends of man,—his best protectors against the ravages of insect tribes.

From the almost boundless catalogue of fruits, we have selected a number comparatively small. Yet even this list is too copious for the gardener on a moderate scale ; for we must repeat the injunction, that excellence, rather than variety, is the object to be aimed at. Among the pears, we have marked with a star those to which we give the preference. Where the ground is limited, it is better to duplicate these, than to take the others.

We give but a short list of apples ; the tree not being so suitable for gardens as the pear.

From the uncertainty which attends the raising of nectarines and apricots, we do not advise the planting of more than one of each sort ; and that should be in some sheltered situation.

DWARF PEARS.

* Bartlett,
* Dearborn's Seedling,
Ott,
Beurré Clairgeau,
* Beurré Diel,
* Livingston Pear,
Dix,
Doyenné Boussock,
* Doyenné Blanc (Virgalieu),
* Duchesse d'Angoulême,
Fondante d'Automne,
* Fulton,
* Louise Bonne de Jersey,

* Oswego Beurré,
* Rostiezer,
* Seckel,
* Sheldon,
Boston,
* Stevens's Genesee,
Tyson,
* Beurré d'Aremberg,
* Easter Beurré,
Beurré Langlier,
Doyenné Goubalt,
* Glout Morceau,
* Lawrence,
* Winter Nelis,
Howell.

DWARF APPLES.

Baldwin,
Melon,
Early Strawberry,
Northern Spy,
Swaar,
Rambo.

PLUMS.

Coe's Golden Drop,
Delicé,
Jefferson,
Lawrence's Favorite,
Green Gage,
Washington.

CHERRIES.

Black Tartarian,
Downer's Late Red,
Great Bigarreau,
Bigarreau Napoleon,
White Bigarreau,
Belle de Choisy,
May Duke,
Reine Hortense.

PEACHES.

Crawford's Early,
    "   Late,
Early Newington,
Early York,
George the Fourth,
Carpenter's Large White.

NECTARINES.

Early Newington,
Stanwick,
Elruge,
Violet Hative.

APRICOTS.

Moorpark,
Breda,
Early Peach.

GRAPES.

Catawba,
Isabella,
Delaware,
Diana.

QUINCE.

Apple Quince.

GOOSEBERRIES.

Houghton's Seedling,
Whitesmith,
Crown Bob,
Early White,
White Eagle, etc.

BLACKBERRIES.

New Rochelle,
Boston High Bush,
Parsley-leaved.

CURRANTS.	RASPBERRIES.
Large Red Dutch,	Red Antwerp,
Large White Dutch,	Yellow Antwerp,
Knight's Early Red,	Brincklé's Orange,
Bang-up (black),	Franconia,
White Grape,	Cushing.
Red Grape.	

The following list comprises a good collection of plants for a flower garden, from 40 to 50 feet square, or of equal area. The list might be greatly extended in number, but not much improved in quality. The addition of some choice bedding plants and annuals (indispensable in every garden) will furnish a supply of flowers during the whole season.

We give the botanical and common names, time of blooming, height of plants, and color of the flower.

DECIDUOUS AND EVERGREEN SHRUBS.

Magnolia purpurea, *Purple Magnolia*, May and June, 8 to 10 feet, purple.

" Soulangeana, *Soulange's Magnolia*, May and June, 8 to 10 feet, pur. and white.

Rhus cotinus, *Venetian Sumach—Fringe tree*, July to Sept., 8 to 10 feet, light purple.

Euonymus Americanus, *American Burning Bush*, 5 to 8 feet; covered with scarlet berries in fall and early winter.

Euonymus latifolius, *Broad-leaved Burning Bush*, 6 feet; red berries in Sept. and Oct.

Rhododendron Catawbiense, *Catawba Rosebay*, July, 8 to 10 feet, purple.

Halesia tetraptera, *Snowdrop*, July, 10 feet, white.

" diptera, *Snowdrop*, July, 10 feet, white.

Viburnum opulus, *Snowball—Guelder Rose*, June and July, 6 to 8 feet, white.

Philadelphus gracilis, *Syringo—Mock Orange*, June and July, 4 to 6 feet, white.

" coronarius, *Syringo—Mock Orange*, June and July, 4 to 6 feet, white.

Crataegus oxycantha rosea fl. pl., *Double Red Hawthorn*, June, 6 to 8 feet, red.

Spiræa Reevesii, *Reeves's Spiræa*, June, 4 feet, white.

" prunifolia pleno, *Double White Spiræa*, June, 4 feet, white.

" trilobata, *Three-lobed Spiræa*, June, 4 feet, white.

Spiræa Douglassii, *Douglass' Spiræa*, August, 4 feet, rose.

"   cratægifolia, *Thorn-leaved Spiræa*, July, 4 feet, white.

"   callosa, a new Spiræa in the style of *Reeves's*, red.

"   thalictroides, *Meadow rue-leaved*—*St. Peter's Wreath*, June and July, 4 to 6 feet, white.

Syringa Josickxa, *Josick's Lilac*, May and June, 6 feet, purple.

"   Persica, *Persian Lilac*, May and June, 6 feet, purple.

Deutzia gracilis, *Graceful Deutzia*, June, 3 feet, white.

"   scabra, *Rough-leaved Deutzia*, June, 6 feet, white.

Pyrus Japonica, *Japan Quince*, June, 4 feet, scarlet.

Weigela (Diervilla) rosea, *Rose-colored Weigela*, May and June, 4 feet, rose.

Chionanthus Virginicus, *Virginia Fringe Tree*, June, 8 to 10 feet, white.

Clethra alnifolia, *Alder-leaved Clethra*, Aug. and Sept., 6 feet, white.

Kalmia latifolia, *Broad-leaved Kalmia, or Sheep Laurel*, June, 4 feet, red.

Calycanthusfloridus *Sweet-scented Shrub*, June, 4 feet, brown.

Amygdalus pumila, *Double-flowering Almond*, May and June, 4 feet, red.

Berberis ilicifolia, *Holly-leaved Berberry*, July, 4 feet, yellow.

"   purpurea, *Purple-leaved Berberry*, June, 4 feet, yellow.

Forsythia viridissima, *Green Forsythia*, May, 4 feet, yellow.

Daphne mezereum, *Sweet-scented Daphne*, May, 3 feet, pink.

Styrax glabra, July, 6 feet, white.

Coronilla emerus, *Scorpion Senna*, May, 3 feet, yellow.

Hibiscus Syriacus, *Rose of Sharon*, Aug. to Oct., 6 feet, various; the variegated leaved and the single red and white. The double varieties are not worth growing.

Lonicera Tartarica, *Upright Honeysuckle*, May, 5 feet, various.

Pæonia moutan, *Tree Pæony*, May and June, 3 feet, purple.

Azalea (in varieties), *Hardy Azalea*, May and June, 3 feet, various.

Aucuba Japonica, *Gold-dust Shrub*, 3 feet, a beautifully marked evergreen plant.

Mahonia aquifolia, *Holly-leaved Berberry*, May and June, 3 feet, yellow.

Cotoneaster microphylla, *Small-leaved Cotoneaster*, 1 foot, white; bears brilliant scarlet berries.

Euonymus Japonicus, *Japan Euonymus*, 4 feet.

Cratægus pyracanthus, *Evergreen Thorn*, 2 feet; bears reddish yellow berries.

HERBACEOUS PLANTS.

Dictamnus rubra, *Red-flowering Dictamnus*, May and June, 2 feet, red.

"   alba, *White-flowering Dictamnus*, May and June, 2 feet, white.

Lychnis chalcedonica, *Scarlet Lychnis*, June to Aug., 2 feet, scarlet.

" viscaria, *Pink Lychnis*, June to Aug., 2 feet, pink.

Delphinium (in varieties), *Perennial Larkspur*, June to Oct., 2 to 4 feet, various.

Phlox " " *Perennial Phlox*, June to Oct., 2 to 3 feet, various.

Pæonia " " *Herbaceous Pæony*, May to July, 2 to 3 feet, various.

Campanula grandiflora, carpatica, etc., *Bellflower*, June to Oct., 2 to 4 feet, various.

Plumbago Larpentæ, *Larpent's Plumbago*, July to Oct., $\frac{1}{2}$ foot, deep blue.

Anemone Japonica, *Japan Anemone*, July to Sept., 1 foot, rose.

Chelone barbata, *Bearded Chelone*, June, 1 to 2 feet, scarlet.

Crucianella stylosa, *Crucianella*, June, $\frac{1}{2}$ foot, pink.

Valeriana rubra, *Garden Valerian*, June and July, 2 feet, red.

" officinalis, June and July, 2 feet, white.

Myosotis palustris, *Forget-me-not*, June to Sept., $\frac{1}{2}$ foot, blue.

Hepatica trilobata, *Liverwort*, May, 1 foot, pink.

Dodecatheon meadia, *American Cowslip*, May and June, 1 foot, red.

Alyssum saxatile, *Golden Alyssum*, May, 1 foot, yellow.

Convallaria majalis, *Lily of the Valley*, May, 1 foot, white.

Aquilegia glandulosa, *Columbine*, June to Aug., 1 to 2 feet, deep blue.

" Canadensis, etc., *Columbine*, June to Aug., 1 to 2 feet, various.

Lupinus polyphyllus, *Perennial Lupin*, June to July, 2 to 3 feet, blue.

" grandiflorus, *Perennial Lupin*, June and July, 2 to 3 feet, blue.

Pyrethrum parthenium (pleno), *Double Feverfew*, June to Oct., 1 to 2 feet, white.

Digitalis purpurea, *Foxglove*, July to Sept., 2 to 3 feet, purple.

" alba, *Foxglove* July to Sept., 2 to 3 feet, white.

Lobelia cardinalis, *Cardinal Flower*, July to Sept., 2 to 3 feet, scarlet.

Yucca filamentosa, *Adam's Thread*, June to July, 2 feet, white.

" gloriosa, June and July, 2 feet, whitish green.

Funkia Japonica, *Day Lily*, August, 2 feet, whitish green.

Œnothera macrocarpa, *Evening Primrose*, June to Sept., 1 foot, yellow.

" Frazerii, etc., July, 2 to 3 feet, yellow.

Stokesia cyanea, *Blue Stokesia*, July, 2 feet, blue.

Spiræa Americana, *Herbaceous Spiræa*, July to Aug., 1 to 3 feet, red.

" filipendula, June to August, 1 to 3 feet, white.

" lobata, June to August, 1 to 3 feet, white.

" Japonica, July to August, 1 to 3 feet, white.

Adonis vernalis, *Spring Adonis*, April, 1 foot, yellow.

Aconitus napellus, *Monk's-hood*, June to August, 3 to 4 feet, blue.

Aconitus speciosus, June to August, 3 to 4 feet, blue.

Monarda didyma, June and July, 2 feet, scarlet.

"   gracilis, June and July, 2 feet, purple.

Lilium candidum,
"   testaceum,
"   speciosum, rubrum et album,   } *Lily*, June to Oct., 2 to 4 feet, various.
"   longiflorum, etc.,

Dianthus (in varieties), *Sweet Williams, Pinks, etc.*, June to Sept., 1 to 2 feet, various.

Statice hybrida, etc., *Sea Lavender, Thrift*, June, 1 foot, various.

Antirrhinum (in varieties), *Snapdragon*, June to Oct., 1 to 2 feet, various.

Dielytra spectabilis, *Dielytra*, June to Sept., 2 to 3 feet, pink.

Chrysanthemums (in varieties), *Artemesia*, Sept. and Oct., 1 to 4 feet, various.

Primula   "   "   *Primrose*, May and June, 1 foot, various.

Iris   "   "   *Iris*, May to July, 1 to 2 feet, various.

Asclepias tuberosa, *Milk Weed*, July and August, 2 to 3 feet, orange red.

Baptisia australis, *Blue Baptisia*, June and July, 2 feet, blue.

Lathyrus latifolius, *a climber*, July to Sept., 4 to 6 feet, purple.

Papaver orientale, *Perennial Poppy*, June and July, 3 feet, reddish yellow.

Pentstemon atropurpureum, *Pentstemon*, July to Sept., 2 to 3 feet, purple.

"   gentianoides, *Pentstemon*, July to Sept., 2 to 3 feet, scarlet.

Polemonium cœruleum, *Greek Valerian*, June, 1 to 2 feet, blue.

Potentilla Hopwoodiana, *Potentilla*, June and July, 1 to 2 feet, yellowish red.

"   atrosanguinea, June and July, 1 foot, red.

Sedum Sieboldii, *Siebold's Stonecrop*, Sept. and Oct., ½ foot, red.

Veronica spicata, *Speedwell*, June to Oct., 1 to 2 feet, blue.

Dracocephalum speciosum, *Dragon's Head*, June to Oct., 2 to 3 feet, pink.

Vinca minor, *Running Myrtle*, July to Sept., ½ foot, blue.

CLIMBERS.

Aristolochia sipho,
Ampelopsis hederacea,
Bignonia radicans,
"   grandiflora,
Clematis in var.,

Hedera helix,
Jasminum humile,
Lonicera in var.,
Menispermum Canadense,
Periploca Græca,
Wistaria sinensis.

CLIMBING ROSES.

Queen of the Prairies,
Baltimore Belle,
Princess Adelaide Moss,
Elegans,
Pride of Washington,
Triumphant.

HARDY PERPETUAL ROSES.

Geant des Battailles, *crimson.*
Antigone, *deep rose.*
Baronne Prevost, *deep rose.*
Augustine Michelet, *deep red.*
Baronne Hallez, *light crimson.*
Caroline de Sansal, *flesh color.*
Comte de Derby, *bright rose.*
Dr. Marx, *carmine.*
Duchess of Sutherland, *pale rose.*
Standard of Marengo, *crimson.*
Lilacée, *rose.*

La Reine, *rosy lilac.*
Mrs. Elliott, *rosy purple.*
Marquise Bocella, *blush rose.*
Madame Trudeaux, *light crimson.*
Madame Laffay, *rosy crimson.*
Prince Albert, *red.*
Rivers, *crimson.*
Bouquet de Floré, *rosy carmine.*
Dupetit Thouars, *crimson.*
Henry Clay, *bright rose.*
Hermosa, *blush.*
Madame Aude, *rose.*
Pierre de St. Cyr, *pale rose.*
Bourbon Queen, *rose.*
Pius IX., *red.*
Malmaison, *flesh color*
Agrippina, *velvety crimson.*
Mrs. Bosanquet, *flesh color.*

Persian Yellow.
Microphylla alba.
Herbemont's Musk Cluster, *white.*